GENDER AND
NATIONAL IDENTITY

Women and Politics in Muslim Societies

GENDER AND NATIONAL IDENTITY

Women and Politics in Muslim Societies

EDITED BY

Valentine M Moghadam

Published for the

UNITED NATIONS UNIVERSITY
WORLD INSTITUTE FOR
DEVELOPMENT ECONOMICS RESEARCH
(UNU/WIDER)

by

ZED BOOKS LTD
LONDON & NEW JERSEY

and

OXFORD UNIVERSITY PRESS
KARACHI

Gender and National Identity was first published for the
United Nations University World Institute for Development
Economics Research (UNU/WIDER), Helsinki, Finland, by
Zed Books Ltd, 7 Cynthia Street, London N1 9JF, UK, and
165 First Avenue, Atlantic Highlands, New Jersey 07716, USA,
and in Pakistan by Oxford University Press, 5 Bangalore Town,
Sharae Faisal, PO Box 13033, Karachi 75350, Pakistan, in 1994.

Cover designed by Andrew Corbett.
Laserset by Philip Daniel.
Printed and bound in the United Kingdom
by Biddles Ltd, Guildford and King's Lynn.

ISBN 1 85649 245 1 Hb
ISBN 1 85649 246 X Pb

In Pakistan
ISBN 0 19 577549 X

Contents

Acronyms and Abbreviations

l'AFMA	Algerian Muslim Women's Association
ALN	National Liberation Army (Algeria)
AWC	Afghan Women's Council
BMNA	Bangladesh Mokti Nirbachan Andalon
CIA	Central Intelligence Agency (US)
DOAW	Democratic Organization of Afghan Women
DRA	Democratic Republic of Afghanistan
FIS	Islamic Salvation Front (Algeria)
FLN	National Liberation Front (Algeria)
KGB	Soviet intelligence agency
MTLD-PPA	Movement for the Triumph of Liberties and of Democracy — party of the Algerian people
OAS	*Organisation de l'Armée Secrète* — underground army of French opposed to Algerian independence and to President de Gaulle's policy
OCFLN	Civil Organization of the National Liberation Front
OPEC	Organization of Petroleum Exporting Countries
PCA	Algerian Communist Party
PDPA	People's Democratic Party of Afghanistan
PLO	Palestine Liberation Organization
RAWA	Revolutionary Association of Women of Afghanistan
SAVAK	Persian acronym for pre-revolutionary secret police [*sazman-e amniat va etellaat-e keshvar*]
UFA	Algerian Women's Union (before independence)
UNESCO	United Nations Education, Scientific, and Cultural Organization
UNFA	National Union of Algerian Women
UNU	United Nations University (based in Tokyo)
UNICEF	United Nations Children's Fund (based in New York)
WIDER	World Institute for Development Economics Research (Helsinki)

Glossary

al-Ard Qablal Ird	Land before Honour — PLO slogan of the 1970s
al-Ird Qablal Ard	Honour before Land — slogan of the Palestinians fleeing Zionism
alpanas	geometric and floral designs (Bengali)
bad-hijab	mal-veiling (Persian), wearing other than regulation Islamic dress
bazaar	market and commercial centre (Iran and Afghanistan)
beechador	unveiled (Persian and Dari)
beehoviyyat	without identity (Persian)
bent el fabrica	'factory girls' (Algeria)
burqa	Afghan veil, tent-like costume covering body and the face
chador	Iranian veil, large sheet wrapped around body and held together by one hand; the head covered but not the face
chadhuri	Afghan chador
chouhada	Algerian word for martyrs of national liberation struggle
conquistadores	Spanish conquerors of the Americas. Also refers to Arab or Muslim conquerors during expansion of Islam
daiates	women proseletyzers (Algeria)
dawla	the Islamic state
dechra	hamlet
Djahilia	(or *Jahilia*), literally, darkness; refers to Arabia before Islam
djebel	war front (Algeria)
djounouds/ *djoundiyates*	soldiers of Algerian National Liberation Army
edaari	office-oriented modern petty bourgeoisie (Iran)
el baraka	beneficence
el Ilm	science
esalat	authenticity (Iran)
fallahat	peasant women
faqih	jurisconsult; supreme legal interpreter in Shiism
farangi	foreigner
fatva	religious decree issued by a person expert in Islamic jurisprudence (Arabic, *fatwa*)

fidaiyates/fiday	urban guerrillas (Algeria); fedayee/n (Iran/Palestine)
fitna	disorder or decay
gharbzadegi	excessive westernization, loss of cultural authenticity (Persian)
gheyrat	Persian-style machismo
hadith	the sayings of Prophet Muhammad recorded by followers; second only to Quran as a basis of Islamic law
Hamas	Movement of the Islamic Society: Palestinian Islamist Group; also Algerian Islamist group distinct from the FIS
hamula	extended family; traditional Palestinian household
haya/hojb	modesty (Iran)
hijab	Islamic modest dress for women
Hizb-e Islami	militant Peshawar-based Afghan opposition group led by Gulbeddin Hekmatyar
Hizb-e Watan	Homeland Party, successor of the PDPA in 1990
ihbat	despair, anomie (Arabic)
intégrisme/grists	North African term for fundamentalism or Islamists
Intifada	Palestinian uprising, West Bank and Gaza, began 1987
jihad	holy war
jilbab	a form of *hijab* (Palestinian)
kachabi	a large and loose coat (Algeria)
Kahina	(real name Dihya); a heroine of North African tribal resistance to the Arab invasion
Khad	Afghan political police
Khalifat	caliphate — the leadership of the Islamic community
Loya Jirga	traditional Afghan tribal council (of men)
mahakem-i famili	family court
mahr	traditional Muslim dower (payments in cash or kind from groom to bride/family), specified in marriage contract
Majlis	assembly; in Iran, Parliament
maquis	an underbrush location where Algerian militants gathered during the National Liberation Movement
marhale-i dovvom	second phase, post-Amin period in the Saur Revolution
massale-i zan	the woman question (Persian and Dari)
medersas	religious schools (Algeria); also, madrassa
mostakbarin	literally, 'the arrogant'; Ayatollah Khomeini's word for the powerful, oppressors, exploiters

mostazaaflin	literally 'humble, meek or wretched'; Khomeini's word for the deprived, oppressed, powerless, exploited
moudarissate	students in the religious girls' schools
moudjahidates	women fighters in the Algerian national liberation struggle
moudjahidines	male fighters in the Algerian national liberation struggle
moussabel/bilates	an urban-based FLN militant (Algeria)
mujahidin	tribal-Islamist opponents of the Afghan government and Saur Revolution, based in Peshawar, Pakistan, in 1980s
mullahs	clerics
nejabat	decency, chastity (Persian)
parti unique	'single party' — referring to the ruling party of Algeria
pieds noirs	Algerian-born Frenchmen
pir	*Sufis* and other missionaries of Islam (South Asia)
purdah	literally, 'curtain'; *hijab* for women in South Asia
Quran	Islamic holy book
quayama	male authority
rebh	interest (banking)
rousari	headdress for women (Persian)
sabt	civil registration
sari	traditional Bengali dress for women
shabab	young Palestinian men
Sharia	Islamic canon law (*Shariat* in Persian and Dari)
sheer-baha	literally 'milk-gift'; a form of dower
Sufis	Islamic mystical sect
tafsir	religious interpretation
Taghouti	literally, 'idol-worshipper'; Khomeini's word for the Shah and royalists
talabeh	student of theology (Persian)
teep	cosmetic red dot on Bengali woman's forehead
ulama	learned religious men; senior clergy
Umma Islamiya	community of believers in Islam
utors	Palestinian women's committees, during the *Intifada*
walwar	brideprice or dower (Pushtun)
zamindar	landlord
zan-e asseel	'culturally authenthic' woman (Persian)
zan-e gharbzadeh	'westoxicated' woman (Persian)

A Note on Transliteration

IN order to facilitate reading by non-specialists, I have adopted a simplified system of transliteration and eliminated all diacritical marks.

In order to respect the distinctiveness of North African terminology, the chapters on Algeria retain the French spelling of certain Arabic words — especially those which denote significant national experiences (for example, *moudjahidates, moudjahidines, fidaiyates, moussabilates, djounouds, djebel, chouhada*).

In the chapters on Iran and Afghanistan, Persian, Dari and Pushtu spellings include the following: *ayatollah, fatva, Khomeini, massale-i zan, gharbzadegi, burqa, walwar, mujahidin, ulama*.

For the sake of consistency, *hijab, jihad, Sharia* and *Quran* are used throughout the book.

Preface and Acknowledgements

THIS book is a product of the UNU/WIDER research programme on women and development, which I have been co-ordinating since March 1990. The research programme has sought to elaborate the gender dynamic of processes of political and economic change in an international perspective. Topics covered include the rise of Islamism and other forms of religious or cultural revival, economic and political restructuring in the former communist world, and patriarchal responses to industrialization and female proletarianization.

The book took shape following the Round Table on Women and Identity Politics, which was held in Helsinki in October 1990, when it became clear that revolutionary societies were a special case of the politics of national identity and gender, and could be treated separately, therefore. The chapters on Iran, Afghanistan, Bangladesh and the Palestinian *Intifada* were prepared for the Helsinki conference, while the chapters on Algeria were commissioned subsequently. Thus, the theoretical and political issues that intersect in this book are the sociology of revolution and national liberation, femininist analysis, and women in the Muslim world.

My deepest thanks go to all the participants of the Round Table on Women and Identity Politics, who have inspired me in more ways than they know, and to my fellow contributors to this book, whose collaboration and friendship have been enriching. I am most grateful to the staff of UNU/WIDER and, particularly, to Arja Jumpponen, who has been involved in this book project since its beginning, tackling the many revised drafts with patience and skill.

Valentine M Moghadam
Helsinki

Chapter 1

Introduction and overview:
Gender dynamics of nationalism,
revolution and Islamization

Valentine M Moghadam

THIS book explores the gender dynamics of political movements from both theoretical and political angles, to demonstrate that nationalism, revolution, and Islamization are gendered processes. The regional focus is North Africa, the Middle East, and South Asia, and the movements examined are predominantly Muslim.[1] Five cases are examined — the experiences of women in the Algerian national liberation movement and in more recent years; the struggle to construct a Bengali national identity and the subsequent creation of Bangladesh; events leading up to revolution and Islamization in Iran; revolution and civil war in Afghanistan; and the Palestinian *Intifada*.

All the authors are from the respective regions, and are activists in addition to being academics. The stakes involved in understanding gender and national identity are consequently theoretical, political, and personal.

The 'Woman Question' in political movements

WHAT is the relationship between nationalism and images of women? What role does the 'Woman Question' play in the discourses and programmes of revolutionaries? What is the link between the consolidation of power by new states and laws about women? Why is the question of women integral to projects of Islamization? What do polemics and policies surrounding veiling and unveiling signify?

These issues are central to an understanding of nationalism, revolution, Islamization, and state-building. But whereas each of these subjects has a prolific body of literature, all are conspicuously parsimonious on issues of gender. Standard texts on nationalism, revolution, Islamization, and state formation are rich in detail on the changing forms of class hierarchies, on national-international linkages, on causes of revolts, and on aspects of state capacity. But very little is explained regarding gender hierarchies, laws about women and the family, and concepts of feminine and masculine. And yet, it is becoming increasingly evident that laws and discourses pertaining to gender are central to the self-definition of political groups and, indeed, signal the political and cultural projects of movements and regimes.[2]

It has also become clear that movements for national liberation and revolutionary states have not always extended principles of autonomy and liberation to women. Far from being the automatic concomitant of national liberation, women's liberation has been frequently regarded as inimical to the integrity and identity of the national group. The most frequently cited example of the disparity between the goals of national liberation and the outcome for women is the Algerian war of independence against the French. And in both the Algerian and the Iranian cases, the fact that women played a crucial role in the revolt did not prevent them from being discouraged, if not barred, from assuming prominence in the public sphere following victory.

If standard disciplinary studies have tended to overlook gender and its articulation with class, the nation-state, and the world system in political processes, women's studies and feminist theory are uncovering the gender dynamics of social change, transition, and political contestation. In recent years feminist scholarship has demonstrated that women frequently become the sign or marker of political goals and of cultural identity during processes of revolution and state-building, and when power is being contested or reproduced. Representations of women assume political significance, and certain images of women define and demarcate political groups, cultural projects, or ethnic communities. Women's behaviour and appearance — and the acceptable range of their activities — come to be defined by, and are frequently subject to, the political or cultural objectives of political movements, states, and leaderships.[3]

We find that, within some political projects, women are linked to modernization and progress. In other cases, women are regarded as central to cultural rejuvenation and religious orthodoxy. In Muslim countries, polemics surrounding veiling and unveiling are tied to different conceptions of the ideal society and to strategies of state-building. In some historical instances, representations of modernity and national progress include the unveiled, educated, and emancipated modern woman, whereas the woman who is veiled signifies cultural and economic backwardness. In other movements, the search for authenticity, cultural revival, and reproduction of the group seems to be incumbent upon re-veiling and family attachment for women. This variability may be explained in terms of the different types of nationalist movements (right-wing, left-wing; religiously-oriented, secular) and in terms of a shifting relationship between nationalist goals and the struggle for women's rights.

Feminism and nationalism

IN a now classic study, Kumari Jayawardena shows how feminism and nationalism in Asia were linked in the nineteenth and early twentieth centuries.[4] The movement towards women's emancipation was acted out against a background of nationalist struggles aimed at achieving political independence, asserting a national identity, and modernizing the society. In some of the cases she studies, resistance to imperialism and various forms of foreign domination provided the essential background. In other cases, exploitative local rulers and traditional patriarchal and religious structures were the principal targets of change. In addition to discussing feminism and nationalism in south, south-east, and east Asia, Jayawardena shows that in Turkey, civilization was equated with women's emancipation; in Egypt, reformism and women's rights were of a piece; in Iran, women's struggles and emancipation from above were parallel movements; and in her brief account of Afghanistan, she notes the failed attempt at women's emancipation and modernization on the part of King Amanullah. In all these, and the other Asian cases, feminism and nationalism were complementary, compatible, and solidaristic.

This has clearly changed. Today, feminists and nationalists view each other with suspicion if not hostility, and nationalism is no longer assumed to be a progressive force for change — the panacea to problems of underdevelopment and social inequality, the path to a healthier and less dominated socio-economic order. In Eastern Europe and the former Soviet Union, nationalism is a retrogressive and disturbing phenomenon in which various national groups and ethnic communities are pitted against each other. In addition, the nationalist project increasingly assigns to women the rather onerous responsibility for the reproduction of the group — through family attachment, domesticity, and maternal roles.[5]

A similar discourse is evident in Islamist movements and in the Palestinian nationalist movement.

Why this change? I believe a clue is provided by Benedict Anderson in his book *Imagined Communities*. Despite the fact that his book does not deal with issues of gender or sexuality, Anderson makes the simple but profound suggestion that nationalism is best viewed not as an ideology but as akin to kinship and religion.[6]

Although I would argue that nationalism was an ideology in Third World countries earlier this century (and in Latin America in the nineteenth century), Anderson's perspective helps explain why, in so many contemporary political movements, women are assigned the role of bearers of cultural values, carriers of traditions, and symbols of the community. If the nation is an extended family writ large, then women's role is to carry out the tasks of nurturance and reproduction. If the nation is defined as a religious entity, then the appropriate models of womanhood are to be found in scripture. Nationhood has been recast in these terms in the latter part of the twentieth century, and this has distinct implications for definitions of gender, for the position of women, and for feminism as an emancipatory project. Women become the revered objects of the collective act of redemption, and the role models for the new nationalist patriarchal family. In Algeria, in spite of the participation of upwards of 10,000 women in the national liberation struggle, their future status was already shaped 'by the imperative needs of the male revolutionaries to restore Arabic as the primary language, Islam as the religion of the state, Algeria as a fully free and independent nation, and themselves as sovereigns of the family'.[7] This is why, *pace* the optimistic vision of Frantz Fanon, the country's independence did not signify the emancipation of women, as Cherifa Bouatta observes in this book. Indeed, Doria Cherifati-Merabtine points out that the FLN (National Liberation Front of Algeria) central organ *El Moudjahid* opposed the term emancipation (identified with the French colonizers) and preferred that of Muslim Woman — which in this context had a political rather than a religious meaning.

Perhaps, then, it is because of the changing nature of nationalism — and certainly because of the evolution of feminism — that the two projects appear less and less compatible. Throughout the world, women are interrogating the assumptions of the nationalist framework and turning to the feminist paradigm for answers to questions about women's roles. This has been occurring in Latin

America, where women in Nicaragua, Peru, Mexico, and elsewhere are no longer satisfied with the subsumption of the 'Woman Question' under the national question. On the issue of reproductive rights and choices in particular, the two projects seem to clash: the pro-natalist bias of so many nationalist leaders inevitably leads to confrontations with women's rights activists. In Nicaragua under the Sandinistas, women's right to abortion was sacrificed as part of the strategy of courting the Catholic hierarchy and owing to demographic concerns resulting from war deaths. Feminists in Nicaragua and their international supporters have now criticized such opportunistic moves.[8] Among Palestinians, assumptions about the compatibility of women's rights and the nationalist agenda are being questioned. As Nahla Abdo observes in this book: 'In almost all liberation movements where women were actively involved, a general reversal of their roles became the fact of life after national liberation and the establishment of the nation-state.' And in light of the growth of Islamist nationalism, Palestinian feminists are beginning to say: 'Yes, we want an independent Palestinian state, but we want it to be democratic, secular, and supportive of gender equality.' And in Algeria, the shift from nationalism to feminism and the rise of militant women's organizations has been a striking feature of the 1980s.

In Algeria, the disillusionment with the nationalist paradigm actually began earlier, and is evident in the observation by the Algerian writer, Assia Djebar, that: 'Women in general ... are conscious of the fact that the Muslim man, however revolutionary he may be within his own union or party or in discharging his civic responsibilities, all too often clings in his domestic life to the old ways'.[9] Djebar explains that a man will still expect his wife to tread the traditional paths and to submit passively to his 'weakened and ineffective authoritarianism'. In turn, he will do relatively little to improve the situation of women, and his wife's silence will aid and abet his inaction. According to Djebar: 'Muslim women are all too often silent, and they appear to be so all the time. The assumption, sometimes overstated, that they exercise a measure of authority behind the scenes is small consolation and one which is generally offered to oppressed minorities'.[10]

Disillusionment with the national liberation model is not limited to Algerian feminists, who blame the *parti unique* for a host of economic and political failures. The challenge has come most forcefully from Islamists, whose rejection of the Algerian state and system extends to an invalidation of the symbols of the national liberation struggle — especially the heroines, the *moudjahidates* — and a repudiation of images of modernity and the West. As in Iran in 1979 and 1980, for Algerian Islamists the most visible expression of unwanted modernization and intrusive Westernization is the unveiled woman — viewed as an alienated being and a cultural traitor. It is she who is at the centre of the contesting discourses, laws, and battles. Counterposed to her is the model of the 'authentic' Algerian and Muslim woman: wearing *hijab*, attached to family and to Islam. In seeking to 'reclaim' Algerian women from 'cultural imperialism', Islamist movements demand legal changes to restore Muslim family law, veiling, sex segregation of sports, and so on.

Thus, a situation has been set up in which women — specifically, middle-class, employed, and modernized women — are at the centre of the contention between Islamist movements and increasingly unpopular states. Women have become the pawns in this political-cultural battleground, and many states have sought to accommodate Islamists and retain their own political power by acquiescing to Islamist demands and passing legislation unfavourable to women. Middle Eastern democrats, feminists, and socialists have responded vigorously. If Muslim women were silent when Assia Djebar was writing, now they most definitely are not. Women's rights activists can be seen and heard in the capital cities of all Muslim countries.

Feminism and socialism

IF the alliance between nationalism and feminism has dissolved, what of the relationship between feminism and socialism? As with nationalism, feminism was on much better terms with socialism earlier in the twentieth century. Socialist and communist parties had an explicitly stated ideological commitment to gender equality, and socialist states also linked women's emancipation to their developmental and modernizing goals. Social transformation and social justice for women were articulated in the Marxist texts and in the programmes of socialists and communists everywhere. Indeed, feminists were greatly inspired by Engels' bold, if somewhat anthropologically and historically flawed, analysis of the origins of the oppression of women.[11] And socialist parties and governments claimed that they, and they alone, could bring about the full emancipation of women.[12] But the hostility of socialists in many developing countries to the demands of 'bourgeois feminists', and the growing evidence from 'actually existing socialism' that women's emancipation still had a long way to go, led to scepticism and eventually a rupture. Although socialist-feminists continue to exist, feminism and socialism seem to be more and more divergent, particularly in the light of the socialists' inability to address themselves to the sexual division of labour at the domestic level, and in view of feminist interest in the politics of difference and identity.[13]

Among Iranians, many former women socialists and communists have now shifted completely to the feminist paradigm, blaming the left for its gender blindness during the Revolution and afterwards. Many of them consider that the principal contradiction in Iran today is not between the state and the people (the populist formulation) or capitalists and workers (the socialist formulation), but between democracy and authoritarianism, and between Islamic patriarchy and women's rights. Two of the chapters in this book include criticisms of left praxis on the 'Woman Question' — those by Cherifa Bouatta on Algeria and Nayereh Tohidi on Iran. However, all the authors here would agree that class-blindness on the part of feminism is as misguided as 'mechanical Marxism's' inattention to gender.

Islamization, women, and cultural relativism

THE emergence and spread of Islamist movements, and the attendant problem of the position of women, have raised important questions regarding modernization, eurocentrism, universalist values, and cultural specificity.[14] These issues are especially salient in the case of Afghanistan, where a tribal-Islamist opposition fought a secular, Marxist-inspired government and its reform programme. But tackling these issues has been complicated by the critique of orientalism, and by a variant of orientalism which views Islamism as a more or less permanent and 'authentic' voice of Muslim societies. How, for example, does one approach the question of veiling? The Islamist answer is predictable, but leftists and liberals alike seem uncertain. Is veiling a free choice of the women? In places where veiling is compulsory, as in the Islamic Republic of Iran, and now in Kabul, the answer is an unambiguous 'no', but what of (re)veiling in Algeria, Egypt, and among Palestinian women? Is veiling an important and necessary symbol of cultural integrity and identity in the face of cultural imperialism? Or could it be that women resort to veiling in the context of intense social pressure if not intimidation? Those of us who grew up in cities (like Tehran), where harassment by men made walking, shopping, or even waiting for a taxi an exasperating and often humiliating enterprise, might understand the desire on the part of women to cover themselves. But then, what does this have to do with cultural identity and integrity?

As the chapters on Iran and Palestine will show, veiling is mandated — largely by men who claim to be upholding religious and national values. And in Algeria, the intimidation of women by Islamist vigilantes in a number of towns and cities is a vivid reminder of the fascistic tendencies inherent in *intégrisme*, or integrative movements. Yet another example is provided by Afghanistan. For years the Afghan *mujahidin* were lauded as courageous freedom fighters battling (Soviet) imperialism. But upon the *mujahidin* take-over of Kabul in May 1992, the very first act of the interim government was to legislate veiling for women. As one journalist wrote from Kabul:

> The most visible sign of change on the streets, apart from the guns, is the utter disappearance of women wearing western clothes. They used to be a common sight. Now women cover up from ankle to throat and hide their hair, or else use the *burqa*, which covers the entire body and has a portcullis-type grille at eye level. Many women are frightened to leave their homes. At the telephone office, 80 per cent of the male workers reported for duty on Saturday, and only 20 per cent of the females.[15]

The *mujahidin* as upholders of national identity and cultural integrity, or as bullies of women?

In fact, the rise of Islamist movements and the turn to (re)veiling should not be seen purely in cultural terms. The causes of Islamist movements are complex and involve political, economic, and cultural factors, including an important external factor — financial and military support from Saudi Arabia, Kuwait, and the Islamic Republic of Iran (and, in the case of Afghanistan, the United States, Pakistan, and China). As I have suggested above and explained elsewhere,[16] the crucial backdrop to the Islamist challenge in the Middle East is widespread disillusionment with the national liberation model, the inability of existing political systems and regimes to live up to the promises of the 1950s-70s, and especially the failure to deliver the benefits of socio-economic development (modernization to some). This raises questions about the gender-specific as well as class-specific effects of socio-economic development.

Let us examine Iran. To the extent that modernization was carried out it benefited women of élite families and a segment of women of the middle class, who welcomed education and employment opportunities, the ability to travel abroad, and the loosening of patriarchal family controls. Other women of the middle class, however, did not view this as liberation. In particular, women from the traditional petty bourgeoisie were confused and angered by contradictory cultural messages, and regarded the need to work as an encumbrance rather than a means toward autonomy and equality. And, of course, all of this was augmented by overwhelming distaste for the Pahlavi regime and all that it stood for. Thus, it would appear that one reason for divisions among women in the Middle East today — the division into pro- and anti-Islamist camps — is the class-specific effects of development on women. It is important to recognize this, for feminists and women-in-development scholars have long debated the relationship between development and women's emancipation, and between employment and gender equality.

It is true that, in the Middle East, socio-economic development and employment opportunities have created a generation of women who, for the first time, do not need family ties for survival, or marriage and children for status. But it is also true that these benefits are unevenly spread among women, and that reactive Islamist movements have singled out precisely the current generation of vocal and visible 'modern' women as an affront to national, cultural, and religious norms. Moreover, it is in the context of economic crisis and social disparities that Islamist movements have emerged and spread, calling for the domestication of women as the solution to the crisis.[17]

Revolution, the state, and women

IN THE light of the foregoing discussion it should be clear that political and cultural projects are gendered, and that 'liberation', 'resistance', and 'autonomy' are invested with gendered meaning. Contemporary nationalist struggles can mean the revival of traditional gender codes which sanctify motherhood and celebrate male power. Struggles around 'authenticity' and cultural identity implicitly or explicitly delineate women's roles and status. Gender politics are at the centre of Islamist movements, where women assume the onerous burden of a largely male-defined tradition and are cast as the embodiment of cultural identity and the custodians of cultural values. Some women regard this as an exalted position, and they welcome it (Islamist women); other women regard it as a form of social control (non-Islamist women).

In revolutions, too, gender struggles as well as class struggles are evident. In examining revolutions and revolutionary states from France to Iran, one finds that the 'Woman Question' assumes a prominent position in revolutionary discourses and in the programmes of the new states.[18] Relevant to the present study is the fact that revolution was claimed by the leaderships of Algeria, Iran, and Afghanistan. As we have already discussed the centrality of women and the family in the Algerian case — and because the Algerian authors in this book regard the Algerian experience to have been a liberation struggle rather than a social revolution — let us illustrate the gender dynamics of revolutionary processes by comparing Iran and Afghanistan.

Iran and Afghanistan share a number of characteristics and experiences. They are neighbouring countries with predominantly Muslim populations that underwent drastic political and social change in the late 1970s. They have both encountered the superpowers in varying ways. In both cases, revolutionaries sought to carry out an audacious programme for political, cultural, and social change, especially in the area of women's rights and family law. In Afghanistan, inasmuch as the new ruling party was comprised of Marxists and socialists, it departed from previous governments, in much the same way that, in Iran, direct clerical rule was unprecedented. However, both the Islamist government in Iran and the Afghan ruling party and government were part of the social fabric and political culture, the product of social changes and modernization in both countries. Like the Islamists in Iran, the Afghan revolutionaries of 1978 were impatient and determined to effect real and lasting change. Most importantly, in both countries, the question of women — or the rearticulation of gender codes and definitions — was central to the programme and vision of the new authorities.

The contrast lies in the type of revolution that took place, the nature of the respective leaderships, the different state capacities, and the specific programme for women that officials in each country adopted. It is commonly understood that Iran experienced a social revolution and Afghanistan a *coup d'état*; that Iran's revolutionary government was popular and representative (endorsed by 98 per cent of the electorate in the April 1979 referendum, according to the government) and that the government of Afghanistan was a minority and unrepresentative regime, buttressed by foreign troops. Yet it was the ostensibly popular and representative government in Iran which passed legislation resulting in loss of status for women, while the 'minority government' next door enacted legislation to raise women's status through changes in family law and marriage customs. In fact, Iran's was a populist revolution and the new leadership are best described as Islamic-populists who constructed a state system based on both theocratic and republican models; Afghanistan's revolutionaries, on the other hand, saw their task as carrying out a national democratic revolution and modernizing the country with the co-operation of the socialist bloc and anti-imperialist countries. Whereas in Iran women were to be covered, in Afghanistan they were to be uncovered. Women's legal status was affected by the two revolutions and the reorganization of state power in very different ways. In a word, women lost legal status in post-revolutionary Iran, whereas in Afghanistan the new state raised women's legal status (or attempted to do so) through two rather bold decrees. Unlike the Islamists in Iran, the Afghan Marxists included a few women in their first government.

The contrast between the two states parallels the divergence in world view and objectives of the movements which arose in opposition to the new states: a modernist and secular opposition to the Islamists in Iran, and a traditional, religious, tribal opposition to the Afghan party and government. Whereas Iran's opposition movement included numerous women activists, intellectuals, spokespersons, and leaders, the Afghan *mujahidin* have never allowed women to assume any positions in their administrative structures. As such the *mujahidin* are fundamentally unlike the liberation or revolutionary movements of Cuba, Algeria, Vietnam, China, Eritrea, Oman, Iran, Nicaragua, El Salvador, and Palestine, where women were/are active as fighters as well as in social services and intellectual work. The absence of *mujahidin* women from the public view also contrasts with the activities of Islamist women in Iran.

The detailed chapters by Tohidi and Moghadam will reveal the differences in the two cases — in particular the very different resource endowments, social structures, depth and scope of development, and state capabilities — but the essential link between them is the paramount position assumed by the 'Woman Question' during the 1980s. Furthermore, at least two theoretical lessons may be drawn from the comparative assessment of women, revolution, and the state in Iran and Afghanistan. One is that a broad-based and popular social revolution in which women massively participate (Iran) does not predict an enhancement of the status of women. Conversely, a 'minority government' may institute genuine reform in the direction of women's emancipation. The explanation lies in the programme of the revolutionary leadership and of the new state.[19] But, although revolutionary ideology and state action are central to an understanding of women's status, the two cases also point to domestic and international constraints faced by states: war, popular resistance, weak central authority, disagreements within the ruling group. Both states have had to modify their original programme on women. In Iran, the 'domestication' of women is no longer exhorted by the authorities, and women are active in public life, but the ruling on *hijab* (veiling) has not altered. In Afghanistan, the bold reform programme had to be suspended owing to civil war and international hostility.

The two cases vividly illustrate the salience of gender in politics, revolutions, struggles around cultural identity, and social movements. In both cases, revolutionaries deemed that something was wrong with society and that addressing *massale-i-zan* (the woman question) would solve the problem. In Iran, the Islamic authorities saw a deep moral and cultural crisis exemplified in 'the naked woman'; to solve the problem, women had to be covered and domesticated. By contrast, in Afghanistan, the secluded, illiterate, veiled woman was seen by the revolutionaries as exemplifying the country's backwardness; consequently, women had to be educated and uncovered. In both cases, revolutionizing society and transforming women were two sides of the same coin.

Organization of the book

THIS book begins with Cherifa Bouatta's study of 'feminine militancy' during and after the Algerian war of national liberation. Bouatta seeks to uncover the 'subjective' side of participation in war and revolution and brings her skills as a social psychologist to bear in her interviews with two *moudjahidates* — Algerian women fighters — regarding their role in the national movement, their views of their role, and their perspectives on the situation of Algerian women today. Both of her subjects are extremely critical of the post-independence status of Algerian women, and Bouatta suggests that one reason for the failure of women activists to attain parity and for the continuation of family patriarchy was that the struggle was precisely one for national liberation, not for social (class/gender) transformation. During the struggle, for example, there was pressure on women fighters to get married and avoid spurious talk of their behaviour. Thus, although 'Houria and Farida have experienced the war and have demonstrated their bravery and their sense of responsibility, the power of the father and the father-in-law wants to continue to reign and to govern their future'.

Chapter 3, also on Algeria, is by Doria Cherifati-Merabtine, who begins by discussing the gender aspects of the war of national liberation. The first half of her chapter is a vivid illustration of the centrality of women to the struggle and the enormity of their suffering, including the mind-boggling sacrifices of women as young as sixteen. These young women, like those of Vietnam, are the stuff of legends, but, as noted in the chapter by Cherifa Bouatta, struggles, revolutions, and movements tend to be seen as male exploits, and not as heroic female feats. Cherifati-Merabtine then goes on to emphasize the disparity between the female militants who had 'acceded to the ranks of subjects of history' and their place in the post-independence leadership, which was 'null'. In the debates on the projects of society, there was no specific commitment to women. Cherifati-Merabtine, like her colleague Cherifa Bouatta, is adamant about maintaining and, indeed, revising the image, symbolism, and real life histories of the *moudjahidates*, especially in the present context of the Islamist challenge and the arbitrary construction of an authentic Algerian Muslim Womanhood by the Islamist movement. Cherifati-Merabtine reports that the Islamist texts have replaced the Algerian *moudjahidat* with the Afghan *moudjahidat*. The irony, as the chapter on Afghanistan will show, is that there is no Afghan *moudjahidat*; this is a mythical construction of FIS (Islamic Salvation Front of Algeria) ideologues. If there is an Afghan equivalent to the Algerian *moudjahidates*, they are the women who took up arms on the side of the Kabul government. The Afghan *mujahidin* never permitted the equivalent of Iran's 'female warriors of Allah'.[20] (If representations are to have any meaning and efficacy, they should at least be accurate!) As an activist and a theorist, Cherifati-Merabtine reveals the stakes involved in representations of women and concepts of the nation. What is more, the question of women in Algeria is 'intertwined with the future of the nation-state and its symbols'.

Salma Sobhan describes the struggle for Bengali national identity and situates the early movement for emancipation of women within the nationalist and anti-nationalist struggle. She then discusses the contention which emerged between East and West Pakistan, following the sub-continent's independence and partition. Disputes revolved around questions of language, script, music, dance, and women's appearance. West Pakistanis accused those in the East of being un-Islamic and excessively influenced by Indian Bengali culture. When civil war broke out, women became a particular target for the Pakistani soldiers who boasted that they would 'convert' East Pakistan through engendering true Muslims. Sobhan notes that a legacy of that trauma is that women's behaviour 'remains the touchstone to determine the purity of Muslim Bengal'. Although Bangladesh was founded as a secular state, the fundamentalists have succeeded in eroding this base. A women's movement has emerged to oppose this fundamentalist vision of Bangladesh, and Sobhan assesses its prospects in her chapter.

The chapters by Nayereh Tohidi and Valentine M Moghadam examine, respectively, the trajectory of the 'Woman Question' in Iran and Afghanistan. Both show how concepts of Woman were associated with political and cultural projects for society. In addition, Tohidi deconstructs the notion of *gharbzadegi*, or Westoxication, to reveal its gender aspects. She discusses further the disconcerting elements of traditional concepts of Womanhood in the writings of leftist and radical men. Perhaps because of such prejudices, the male-dominated left was not especially attentive to women's rights issues, and tended to dismiss the clerical exhortations on veiling — and feminist concerns about them — as a 'superstructural' phenomenon lacking the urgency or relevance of the struggle against imperialism and capitalism.[21] Tohidi ends by discussing the emergence of Islamist women activists in contemporary Iran.

The chapter on Afghanistan by Moghadam describes how difficult it has been for reformers, modernizers, and revolutionaries to tackle the question of the status of women in the context of an underdeveloped and patriarchal society and weak state authority. In a more political vein, the author argues against support for national liberation movements which lack a progressive social programme and occlude questions of class and gender hierarchies.

Nahla Abdo's chapter examines feminism and nationalism in the context of the Palestinian *Intifada* and the role of women and women's organizations within it. She distinguishes between 'official nationalism' (that of a state) and 'popular nationalism' (the grassroots version), and although especially critical of the former, recognizes the limitations of the latter, especially for women's autonomy and equality, and in the light of the leadership's pro-natalist sentiments. Following an historical survey of Palestinian women's activism, Abdo draws from her recent fieldwork and interviews to describe the emergence of women's organizations and a heightened gender consciousness during the *Intifada*. She is convinced that, at least as far as the Palestinian movement for national liberation is concerned, there is 'No Going Back' for women. One can only hope that this is so.

Notes

1. This must be qualified in the case of the Palestinians, who are Christian and Muslim alike.

2. See, for example, Nira Yuval-Davis and Floya Anthias (eds.) and contributors, *Woman-Nation-State* (London: Macmillan, 1989); and Deniz Kandiyoti (ed.) and contributors, *Women, Islam and the State* (London: Macmillan, 1991).

3. See Hanna Papanek, 'The Ideal Woman and the Ideal Society: Control and Autonomy in the Construction of Identity', in V M Moghadam (ed.) *Identity Politics and Women* (Boulder, Colo: Westview Press, 1994). See also Valentine M Moghadam, 'Revolution, Islam and Women: Sexual Politics in Iran and Afghanistan', in Andrew Parker, Mary Russo, Doris Sommer, and Patricia Yaeger (eds.) *Nationalisms and Sexualities* (New York: Routledge, 1992), pp. 424-46.

4. Kumari Jayawardena, *Feminism and Nationalism in the Third World* (London: Zed Books, 1986).

5. See Valentine M Moghadam (ed.) and contributors, *Democratic Reform and the Position of Women in Transitional Economies* (Oxford: Clarendon Press, 1993). See also Maxine Molyneux, 'The Woman Question in the Age of Perestroika', *New Left Review* 183 (September/October 1990), pp. 23-49; and Ruth Pearson, 'Questioning Perestroika: A Socialist-feminist Interrogation', *Feminist Review* 39 (Winter 1991), pp. 91-6.

6. Benedict Anderson, *Imagined Communities: Reflections on the Origin and Spread of Nationalism* (London: Verso, 1983), p. 15. An excellent elaboration of this thesis for Algeria is by Peter Knauss, *The Persistence of Patriarchy: Class, Gender and Ideology in Twentieth Century Algeria* (Boulder, Colo: Westview Press, 1987). See especially his Introduction.

7. Knauss, op. cit., p. xiii.

8. See, for example, Maxine Molyneux, 'Mobilization Without Emancipation? Women's Interests, State, and Revolution', in Richard R Fagen, Carmen Diana Deere, and José Luis Coraggio (eds.) *Transition and Development: Problems of Third World Socialism* (New York: Monthly Review Press, 1986), pp. 280-302. See also Virginia Vargas, 'The Women's Movement in Peru: Streams, Spaces, and Knots', *Working*

Paper, Institute of Social Studies, The Hague, 1990. For a more sympathetic view, see Norma Stoltz Chinchilla: 'Marxism, Feminism, and the Struggle for Democracy in Latin America', in *Gender & Society* 5 (3) (September 1991), pp. 291-310; and 'Revolutionary Popular Feminism in Nicaragua: Articulating Class, Gender and National Sovereignty', *Gender & Society* 4 (3) (September 1990), pp. 370-97.

9. UNESCO Courier, August-September 1975, p. 28.

10. Ibid.

11. Frederick Engels, *Origin of the Family, Private Property, and the State*, especially the Preface to the First Edition, 1884. *Marx and Engels: Selected Works*, Vol. 3, pp. 191-334 (Moscow: Progress Publishers, 1970).

12. See Maxine Molyneux, 'Socialist Societies: Progress Toward Women's Emancipation?' *Monthly Review* 34 (3) (July-August 1982), pp. 56-100; and Sonia Kruks, Rayna Rapp and Marilyn B Young (eds.) *Promissory Notes: Women in the Transition to Socialism* (New York: Monthly Review, 1989).·

13. See, for example, Zillah Eisenstein, 'Reflections', in Kruks, Rapp, and Young (eds.) *Promissory Notes*, pp. 333-37. As part of her critique of socialist theory and practice, she writes: 'Radical pluralism is not a part of a socialist theory of sex equality because heterogeneity, particularly individual, and specifically bodily difference(s), are not theorized as a distinct aspect of social relations' (p. 335). For a critique of such a feminist perspective, see Jenny Bourne, 'Homelands of the Mind: Jewish Feminism and Identity Politics', *Race & Class* (29) 1990, pp. 1-24; and Lynne Segal, 'Whose Left? Socialism, Feminism and the Future', in Robin Blackburn (ed.) *After the Fall* (London: Verso, 1992) pp. 274-86 — both salutary analyses of the problems and prospects. I would like to add, with regard to the relevance of socialist/Marxist theory, that the sexual division of labour within the household can be explained, particularly within the production/reproduction framework, and in a way remarkably consistent with Engels' critical analysis of the function of the family, especially his comments in the 1884 Preface to *Origin of the Family, Private Property and the State*.

14. See, for example, Mona Abaza and Georg Stauth, 'Occidental Reason, Orientalism, Islamic Fundamentalism', *International Sociology* 3 (4) (December 1988); V M Moghadam, 'Against Eurocentrism and Nativism: A Review Essay on Samir Amin's Eurocentrism and Other Texts', *Socialism and Democracy* 9 (Fall/Winter 1989), pp. 81-104. See also Bill Brugger and Kate Hannan, *Modernisation and Revolution* (London: Croom Helm, 1983), for a critique of 'eurocentric' approaches to the Islamic aspects of the Iranian Revolution.

15. Derek Brown, 'New Afghanistan Carries on Grisly Game of the Old', *The Guardian*, 4 May, 1992, p. 7.

16. V M Moghadam, 'Islamist Movements and Women's Responses', *Gender & History* 3 (3) (Autumn 1991), pp. 268-86.

17. For a further elaboration of this, see Fatima Mernissi, 'Muslim Women and Fundamentalism: Introduction to the Revised Edition', *Beyond the Veil: Male-Female Dynamics in Modern Muslim Society* (Bloomington: Indiana University Press, 1987); Valentine M Moghadam, *Modernizing Women: Gender and Social Change in the Middle East* (Boulder, Colo: Lynne Reinner Publishers, 1993), especially chs 4 and 5. See also Nahid Toubia (ed.) *Women of the Arab World* (London: Zed Books, 1988), especially the chapter by Nawal El Saadawi, 'The Political Challenges Facing Arab Women at the End of the 20th Century', pp. 8-26.

18. I have previously discussed this in 'Revolution En-gendered: Notes on The Woman Question in Revolutions', paper presented at the XII World Congress of Sociology, Madrid, July 1990. See also *Modernizing Women*, op. cit., chapter 3.

19. This helps to explain the impact on women of the '1989 revolutions' in Eastern Europe despite the massive participation of women in the dissident movements. Everywhere, the majority of the newly unemployed are women; they have lost many of the social benefits they previously enjoyed, and now constitute a disproportionately small percentage of decision-makers in the new political structures, which includes parliaments.

20. The term is from the book by Minou Reeves, *Female Warriors of Allah: Women and the Islamic Revolution* (New York: E P Dutton, 1989).

21. On this issue, see also V M Moghadam, 'Socialism or Anti-Imperialism? The Left and Revolution in Iran', *New Left Review* 166 (November/December 1987), pp. 5-28.

Chapter 2

Feminine militancy: *Moudjahidates* during and after the Algerian war

Cherifa Bouatta

THE war for national liberation has been the subject of numerous studies with historical, sociological, and political perspectives. We believe, however, that entering the war also had psychological and socio-psychological dimensions that have been underestimated, or even ignored, in the studies of the Algerian war.[1] Is it, perhaps, irrelevant to raise psychological problems when it is the history of a whole people that is involved? In this case, the investigation should focus on the problematic posed by the colonization/decolonization phenomena.

Furthermore, these studies (mainly those carried out by Algerians and French) are rarely undertaken by participants in the war. Some *moudjahidines*, such as Hocine Ait Ahmed and Yacef Saadi, have written their memoirs.[2] Others have gone further and attempted to elaborate some theorization.[3] Two observations can be formulated about these writings: (1) in general, there are not many; and (2) they are the discourses of men, about the adventures of men. The female *moudjahidates*[4] have produced no discourses and no formalization about their experience of the war. If it is true that the task of writing and the task of theorization require some distancing, some standing back, they also require an education and a training that participants in the war do not always possess. It remains that it is the men who have given evidence; the women have not.

It should also be emphasized that the discourse developed in Algeria after independence concerning the women's project are male discourses, both in the official documents (the two national charters and the family code, for example) and in the media. The men occupy the management and decision-making posts, and legislate and promulgate laws relating to the status of the women. In other words, the only voices concerning the war and the feminine questions are masculine voices. The following two facts provide a summary:

The absence of the psycho-sociological dimension as a parameter in entering the war for individuals;

The discourses concerning the war ignore the feminine question on one hand, and they are masculine elaborations, on the other hand. Hence, the problem of the silence of the *moudjahidates*.

A point of history: forms of feminine struggle

WOMEN were involved in the war in a variety of ways. They went into the *maquis*[5] as nurses or as fighters: they were *moudjahidates*. The *fidaiyates*,[6] those who planted bombs stayed in the city; others, and sometimes the same ones, carried the messages, the money, and weapons. The 'Battle of Algiers' could not have taken place without these women.[7] However, the majority of women took part in the war more discreetly. These anonymous women provided the supply and logistic corps of the war; they provided the medical care, did the cooking, and hid the passing *moudjahidines*. It was these women who were harassed by the French soldiers because their sons or husbands had gone to the war. They also had to put on the 'apron'[8] and integrate the '*Fatma*'[9] group because the men were absent and they had to meet the needs of their families. It was these women, too, who searched for missing persons or for prisoners, wandering from camp to camp, from prison to prison, and always on the look-out for any information that might help with their search. This tragic and desperate role, reinforced by bonds of attachment and love between human beings, has been immortalized by the Algerian film-maker Lakhdar Hamina in *Le Vent des Aures*.[10]

When, following numerous episodes of humiliation by the French authorities, the woman, mother or wife managed to discover the place of detention, another adventure began: that of the prisoner's basket. It had to be filled, which was not easy, and carried, after obtaining the right to visit from the French administration. It was the women who, in defiance of the French army, took to the streets on 11 December 1961 to repudiate colonial propaganda claiming that the war concerned only a minority of Algerians. Their action demonstrated the attachment of the Algerians to the National Liberation Front (FLN) and to independence. This massive emergence of women on to the public scene impressed international opinion.

Women's roles in the war thus ranged from the most spectacular to the most discreet, but whatever the part played it created additional problems for the women who were often impoverished and lived a difficult and dangerous daily life.

The Algerian war was a decisive turning point in the struggle of colonized countries. It was a demonstration of the power of the people, in the sense that it gave the colonized the status of heroes in history. For the duration of the war, the women had become heroines, among whom the most famous were the three Djamilas — Djamila Bouhired, Djamila Boumaza, and Djamila Boupacha — and Hassiba Ben Bouali.[11]

The women's aim and approach

THE foregoing has shown that women played an integral part in the war. Our focus now will be not on the number of women involved or the nature of their participation, but on how particular women explain their involvement, their motivations, and relate their experience of the war.

How do certain women cross the line and enter a war? Clearly, the simple answer would be that there was a need to liberate the country, support and sometimes replace the men, in order to end the colonial domination. But we want to go further and attempt to discover whether, for the women, these reasons are related to other more specific ends connected with the status of their sex.

Did the *moudjahidates*, being women, have other motivations and aspirations, besides independence, support and replacement of the men? Was their involvement in the war the result of a breakdown in the family order? Did they have any emancipation aims? And today, after acquiring independence, what do they think of their experience in the war and of the feminine condition in general?

These questions are rarely raised in the studies related to wars and revolutions. We have deliberately chosen to promote them in order to define the experience of certain women who took part in the war. In this way we come to apprehend ideas, thoughts and sentiments — in brief, subjectivities.

Our decision is not arbitrary. It is a common practice to ignore individual and subjective factors — in our opinion this leaves a gap. Even if a study of this particular dimension does not reveal the whole meaning of the movement concerned — war or revolution — nevertheless, the meaning is enriched by giving it a psychological depth and illuminating the humanity that animates it. Furthermore, in the contemporary scientific world, the study of ideas and thought has been rehabilitated, signifying a break with a certain type of mechanical Marxism that stigmatized consideration of *ideas* [12] as philosophism and bourgeois idealism.

Our approach encompasses several aspects. One consists of listening to women's accounts of their entrance into the war, focusing on how they interpreted the important events that they lived through, and in which they participated. It is also a way of ending the silence of the *moudjahidates* and restoring a feminine voice on the war. Answering the questions we formulated will deliver the subjective dimension of the feminine participation in the war, which is vital to our reflections.

The method used is a non-directed discussion consisting of one or more themes around which the subject is invited to talk freely. Our role was to maintain the discussion in line with the object of this study. This approach may be criticized for evading any theoretical content but by conducting the procedure on two levels — one concerns the gathering of information through discussion, and the other its analysis to obtain answers to the questions formulated — this objection is overcome.

However, the technique does present at least two disadvantages: the accounts are too long to include in their entirety within the limits of this chapter, therefore only short extracts are included for illustration.

The themes proposed — which form the matrix of the discussion — relate to three moments, which we have called *the founding moments of the subject's itinerary*, since they structure their individual history. These are: before the war; during the war; and after the war.

The time used by the subjects was not chronological time. In fact, the oral discourses are far from following a Before, a During, and an After sequence. On the contrary, the subjects tend to mix the times: they speak of today and then talk of the war or events related to before the war. Therefore, it was necessary to reorganize their answers according to the three selected times to make them more coherent.

We selected two women for the purpose of this work.[13] The first, Houria, was in the *maquis*. After independence she worked as a civil servant. She retired recently, aged 51, relatively early for retirement, but the years in the *maquis* are counted as working years. Houria has three daughters whom she brought up alone. She lives with her third daughter. It must be noted that Houria got a divorce just after independence.

The second, Farida, was a liaison agent in the FLN's France federation. She is 47, married with four children and lives with her family in a big house near the capital. She decided to give up working five years ago, but is still very active: she is a militant member of a women's association whose objective is equality between men and women.

The choice of two women precludes any idea of generalization. However, our primary interest is not the discovery of *sociological laws* concerning all the women engaged in the war, but rather to determine and define some socio-psychological elements of this feminine participation.

A major theoretical definition is essential before proceeding in order to further clarify our thoughts. The facts related to us, and the opinions of the subjects concerning the periods before and during the war, are to be situated in what the psychoanalysts call *l'après-coup*. We make use of this notion of *après-coup* because the reported accounts are not to be considered as a spontaneous and strict record of reality, whether in terms of factual accounts or in recalling ideas. The war ended in 1962, and the data was collected 29 years later. In this case, it is clear that the experiences of war, and the ideas and sentiments that accompany them have been reorganized and reordered according to the new living conditions. Moreover, it is not real life that is ordered: psychological processes intervene selectively to allow the subject to re-elaborate past experiences, and to give them new significance.

The three themes proposed are elaborated as follows:

1. **Before the war**: type of family, mode of life, relations with family members. The idea of entering the war, the elements determining the *passage à l'act*.

2. **During the war**: the family's reaction to the daughter's involvement in the war. The role she played and the nature of the relationships with the other people taking part in the war (men and women).

3. **After the war**: Algeria's independence. Appreciation of the experience of the war. Relationship with the companions in the struggle. Current aspirations. Point of view on the feminine condition. The reason for the social eclipse of the *moudjahidates*.

Elements of the answers

DID women's entry into the war signify a breakdown of the patriarchal system that structures the Algerian family, and did it signify the arrival of a new social order? According to Frantz Fanon the answer is in the affirmative.[14] Indeed, he considers that the Algerian revolution propelled to prominence an age category (the young) and a sex category (the women). These categories are subordinated in the patriarchal system where power resides with adult men.

Thus, according to Fanon, the war was to shake the patriarchal familial edifice. From that time, as a result of war, the social rules are in the hands of the young and the women; the nature of the relationships between old and young, and between the sexes, is seriously shaken. Fanon argues that the war signifies the beginning of the end of the patriarchal system.

The course of events was to invalidate Fanon's optimistic theses. Of course, in the wake of independence, the women were present in parliament, in the mass organizations, and in management. This presence was minimal, even symbolic, but it was an innovation that could have been the beginning of an evolution of the feminine condition. But the women were very quickly removed from the political sphere and confined to a women's organization, the UNFA (Union Nationale des Femmes Algériennes) under the guardianship of the single political party: the FLN. The role of UNFA was insignificant: its activities limited to opening sewing classes for women and supporting the FLN's decisions. In fact, its impact within the female population was non-existent. Further, many women came to accuse this organization of playing into the hands of those in power, and denied it the right to represent them. A slow regression of the feminine condition was therefore taking place. This situation culminated in the adoption of the Family Code in July 1984. The text of this law, inspired by the *Sharia*, officially establishes women in a position of inferiority, and establishes the dominance (*quayama*) of men in matters concerning marriage, divorce, inheritance, and so on. From 1984, Algerian law legitimizes men's domination of women.

It must be emphasized that the promulgation of the Family Code was the result of a long struggle between women (the 'modernist' movement *vs* the traditionalists) around the judicial status of women. In 1963, shortly after independence, there was a failed attempt to codify relations between men and women within the family. Other attempts were made in 1965, 1970, and 1973 but, given the divergences between the different groups, success was delayed until July 1984. It was in opposition to the Family Code and to its vision of the gender that women began to organize and mobilize. Indeed, a women's organization calling for equality between men and women in the eyes of the law was created in May 1985. Significantly, this organization was outside the influence of the FLN.

The text of this code, based on the *Sharia*, is supposed to be the preservation of the Algerian Muslim identity. According to this logic, the Algerian identity will be under threat if equality between the sexes was permitted. The promulgation of this code introduces us to the feminine dilemma in Algeria where its women are faced with an irreconcilable legal dualism: on the one hand, and in reference to the role of women during the war of national liberation, they are the equal of men, according to certain laws. This is the case in the constitution and in labour legislation. On the other hand, the Family Code, in reference to Islam and in order to guarantee the national identity, institutionalizes the inferior status of women. This is women's present legal situation. Their social status is no more comfortable. Despite some incursions in the world of work, and in the field of scholarship, the patriarchal ideology remains dominant and dictates relationships between the sexes. The rise of the Islamist movement reinforces and legitimizes (through the manipulation of religion) discrimination against women in the broad social spheres.

The Family Code remains a most controversial text of law. Some women's organizations demand amendments to some of its articles that are adjudged too discriminatory (those related to marriage and divorce). Others demand abrogation of the code and its replacement by civil laws. The Islamists, on the other hand, want to retain it: they consider that the code is the only single law in Algeria that tends towards the ideal of the *Sharia*.

This schematic survey of the feminine condition after independence contradicts the optimistic vision of Fanon and challenges the idea that the country's independence automatically signifies women's emancipation.

Returning to our aim, let us examine how relationship to the familial patriarchal order is handled at the level of the individual.

Before the war

HOURIA comes from a very poor rural family consisting of six children. Her father died when she was six. 'All of us were living in a single room.'[15] Her twelve-year-old brother 'did odd jobs to bring some money into the house. It was misery.' At the age of fourteen, Houria was taken out of school. 'I had the housekeeping to do, the kitchen, going to the well for the water. When the French were here, the school was not for us.'

Farida is from a family of ten children. The family emigrated to France in 1948 where the father worked in a factory. 'I was a model schoolgirl. My parents insisted on us having irreproachable behaviour at school. We must not give a bad image of the Algerians.'

The Passage à l'Act

HOURIA explains: 'You know, it was misery at our house, all around me ... I was unhappy. I hated everything ... I was suffocating. My mother was very, very hard. I could not raise my eyes to her. During the eight-day strike,[16] the French surrounded our district. They took away the able-bodied men and packed the older men and women on one side and the young girls on the other. We were frightened ...[17] We had heard that there were women in the *djebel*[18] and we thought that we would go too. We were determined to go. The other girls did not have the opportunity to do it. I had a cousin who was a *moussabel*.[19] I told him of my desire to go. Initially, he refused, saying: "What will your mother say?" But he ended up accepting. One day, he brought me some money and told me: "You are responsible for buying medicines for the *djounouds*."[20] I used to put on the veil at that time. I used to hide my veil and shoes under a tree and tell my mother that I was going to visit a neighbour. I went around the chemists and bought the medicines. My cousin used to come and collect them. He took me once to my aunt's where I had to wait for some *moudjahidines*. When they came we served them some food and I told my cousin that he must tell them about me. They said that I had to wait for their leaders. Another time, my cousin took me to see another leader who said that I had to wait for the return of Si[21] Mohamed, who was the chief at that time.

'After a long wait, my cousin took me to see the person in charge of the *maquis*. I told him of my desire to join them. He told me: "What will your parents think? You are too young. The *djebel* is very hard". I replied: "It is too late for me, I cannot go back to the house, I would rather die." They took me with them. I was seventeen then.'

FARIDA explains: 'My neighbour was a liaison agent and she needed a cover. The brothers[22] decided that I must accompany her everywhere. I was twelve. They told me that if I said anything, they would kill me. I was not frightened. My father was a militant in the FLN, the brothers used to meet in our house and used to say that the country was living under slavery and that it must be liberated. I used to listen to their conversations. So, when they asked me to accompany my neighbour, I found it normal to do something to participate in the liberation of my country. You know, I was very aware of the war. Everybody in our house was a militant. My mother used to cook for all the brothers that used to come to our house; she used to hide all sorts of things for them. Hence, my participation was completely natural.'

During the war

FOR Houria, as in the *djebel*, the *maquis* meant much travelling, journeys from *dechra* [hamlet] to *dechra*, from region to region, long marches that lasted weeks with very short breaks. Bleeding feet, exhausted bodies, and all sorts of privations. Encounters with the people and the women of the *dechra*. It was also the time of her marriage: 'Some time after going to the *djebel*, the person in charge proposed that I should marry a *djoundi* called Ali. I refused, I was too young. But they convinced me. They also told me: "You'd better get married otherwise you may be sent to Tunisia".' She adds: 'At that time, many female *moudjahidates* were sent to Tunisia and a number died at the border.'[23]

Houria continues: 'I told them: "What will my parents and family say?" The person in charge replied: "Here, we are the authority, we will take care of your family." Sometime later, I got the approval of my brother. I got married to Ali. We lived together for three months and we were married for a year; most of the time, we were not together. My husband died in 1959, during an encounter with the French. I was not with him. I had a daughter by this marriage.

'Just before my husband died, I went to stay with my mother-in-law. My husband came to see me one day and then went back to the *maquis*. After a while I returned to the *djebel* and I was told my husband had been wounded and was very ill. He was suffering a lot and there were no medicines to treat him.'

When asked about the nature of the affective and sexual relationships with her first husband (Houria remarried), she began by refusing to answer: 'No, we don't talk about that.' When we insisted, she finally said: 'Our relations were rare. It was not possible in the *djebel*, with the *djounouds*, sometimes we were alone in a *dechra* ... He was jealous, you know our men, the *djounoud* liked me and I liked them too, I was the only woman among them, I was their sister. He was not pleased with it, it made him angry ... When he died, I was four months pregnant. I spent all my pregnancy in the *djebel*, I used to wear a *kachabia* [24] to hide my pregnancy. I gave birth in a *dechra*. The *moudjahidine* named my baby daughter Djamila, in tribute to Djamila Bouhired. My daughter stayed with me for two months, but it was very hard, the living conditions ... In fact, she caught a throat infection which developed into a cardiac illness, so I sent her to her grandmother.

'I married for a second time. During Operation Challes,[25] we were completely isolated, we did not have contacts with the population. The people in charge told me: ''You must get married.'' They married me to a militant who was in the city. He arranged our marriage using the documents of his dead cousin. With this new identity, I could move around, distribute the money to the widows of the *chouhada* [26] and to the wives of the *moudjahidines*. Afterwards, I learnt that the French were looking for me, so I stopped my trips.'

FARIDA: 'I had been accompanying Malika for a long time on her trips. But once I got older, I was given missions too. In this way, I covered part of France, I had been to Germany, Belgium. I had to go unnoticed, be taken for a French person, so as not to arouse any suspicions, since anybody who looked like an Arab was searched and arrested. So, I used to put on make-up and dress in the French way.

'As an Algerian, I had to succeed in school, I had to show to the French that we were able to succeed. When I got my secretarial diploma, I used to type letters, tracts .... I also distributed them.

'Every time the police arrested a brother, I was told to send him letters, to visit him in prison and pretend I was his fiancée, to make it look as if he did not have any links with the FLN.

'Sometimes, I carried weapons. Once, I gave a gun to a brother who had an action to carry out. He was wounded. I carried him through the city to our house. One of my brothers was still a baby at that time. When I had to carry documents through the city, I used to hide them under his push-chair.

'Afterwards, my father was banned from the north of France. They transferred us to a camp in Marseilles.'

Relations with companions in the war

With the women:

HOURIA: 'I did not meet many women in the *djebel*. At the beginning, I was with Torkia, a married woman. Two other *moudjahidates* were supposed to join us. One was killed and the other arrested during an encounter with the French on their way. I had also been with another sister for a while, but people said she was not good.[27] I used to meet women in the *dechra*, eat with them, sleep in their houses, and, when I had to leave, they all used to give me something: eggs, honey, bread.

'Many women in the *dechras* were amazed to see me alone with a group of men; it was unusual for them.'

FARIDA: 'We did not have the right to meet, or to know each other. We used to pass each other in missions only. For example, I would have to deliver something to some woman, somewhere, I did not know her name or anything. I passed many women like this.'

With the men:

HOURIA: 'There was total respect between us, it was not like today, we were really united, never a word out of place. The women were really respected. In the *djebel*, we were all equals; the *djounouds* did their washing, they used to cook; I used to carry weapons like them.'

FARIDA: 'We were as real brothers and sisters. We respected each other a lot.'

Reactions of the family:

HOURIA: 'I left the house, I went to the *djebel* without the consent of my mother. She would never have allowed me to leave the house. She learned about it later.'

FARIDA: 'It was because my father was a militant and our house was a refuge that the brothers asked me to help them. At twelve, it was my father who told me: "You are going to accompany Malika in her trips."

'My brother was worried about what other people will say. In Marseilles, we were among Algerians and Moroccans. My brother wanted to prevent me from going out. He used to tell me: "People see you with men." It was the intervention of my father that allowed me to continue my militant activities. My brother was also a militant in the FLN. My parents used to tell me: "You must be very careful. You must be irreproachable and show to everybody that the Algerian girls are serious".'

Political training and discussions:

HOURIA: 'We talked about getting the French out, that is all. We talked jokingly about the future but we did not always believe in it.' Houria admits that the political problems and the feminine question were not part of her thoughts. She says: 'When we used to go through the *dechras* and see the state of destitution, the misery of the population, we used to say to ourselves that this will change when the French are out.'

FARIDA: 'We had seminars on politics after independence. During the war, I used to think that I will go back to my country to participate in its development.'

After the war: Independence

HOURIA: 'In 1962, I met my husband, but I was very unhappy with him. He used to disappear for days, going with other women, while I was locked in the house. So, we divorced,[28] and I started looking for a job. But I could not do anything, I had no qualifications. I ended up finding a job with the help of the *moudjahidines*.'

FARIDA: 'I wanted to go back to Algeria, the country of the dreams of my mother. I wanted to go back to the country I fought for. My father refused categorically, saying: "You must get married first." I met my future husband in a seminar organized by the FLN in France. I got married and went back to Algeria.'

HOURIA: 'When I came back from the *djebel*, my mother was very proud of me. Everybody celebrated my return. The women wanted my clothes for *El baraka*,[29] to help sterile women to have babies, and women who had sick children hoped that my clothes would bring healing. Today, I am well respected in the family, everybody listens to me and asks for my advice.

'When I started work, my colleagues did not believe that I used to be a *moudjahidat*. They did not have any consideration for me. One day, I met Si Oman (a commander in the *djebel*) at my workplace. He recognized me immediately. He said in front of all my colleagues: "How is the *moudjahidat*?" We chatted about the past, my work, I told him about the difficult working conditions; he talked to my boss and then things got a little better. This was how my colleagues finally understood that I was a *moudjahidat*.'

FARIDA: 'My mother had always described Algeria as a paradise where people were nice, generous ... I had always believed her.

'When I went back to the country, my dream vanished. I had to live with my parents-in-law. I was locked up. It was out of the question to work, to have a profession. Nobody spoke to me. My husband's family did not accept my presence, they have never accepted me. Many times I contemplated suicide.

'A friend persuaded my husband that I should work. So I started working. My father-in-law expelled us (my husband and myself) from his house: he could not stand the idea of me working.

'In 1963, I took part in the congress of the FLN. After that, I worked in the political bureau of the FLN. I also taught secretarial skills at a school in Algiers.

'I refused to join the UNFA. I think the women of this organization are not very serious. I knew them very well, I could see what they were up to and I did not agree with their ideas or with their methods.'

Today

Relations with companions in the struggle:

HOURIA: 'Sometimes, I meet some women that I knew during the war. We are happy to meet. But that is all. Besides, in the region where I was, there were not many women, and they were all commanded by men, they could not do anything. Some of them are like me: they run after their subsistence.

'Sometimes I meet with the *moudjahidines* [males]. They have helped me, they have made documents for me, they found me a job. My first job was as an orderly in a hospital. It was very hard and very far from where I lived. I also had to work night shifts which was virtually impossible because of my children. It was the brothers who got me another job. You know, the *moudjahidates* receive no consideration. Personally, I gained nothing on the material side. I had to work really hard to bring up my three daughters.'

FARIDA: ' I see some of the women of the French federation. But they are all very busy. The women have not played their role after independence. They were only interested in power. Some would have done anything for power. They became object women. The men have blocked their way. They did not want the women with them.'

Appreciation of the experience of war:

HOURIA: 'I am very proud. I regret nothing. They were my years of happiness. It was the fraternity, the respect, I can't tell you.'

FARIDA: 'I am very proud of my past. I think that the women should have continued the struggle. We would not be in this situation today.'

Views on the feminine condition:

HOURIA: 'What hurts me, what I cannot get into my head, is the women colonized by men.[30] The man gives five or six children to the woman, then leaves her with a bag of potatoes and spends his time outside. The woman is really humiliated. If I could do anything, I would have changed all this. The woman accepts this, she does nothing to change her situation. It is her fault.
    'The women follow the FIS.[31] They listen to it while the FIS wants to bury them alive. All this because the government does nothing to improve the fate of women. When I see women engineers and doctors, I think that it is thanks to us that the women can today have interesting jobs, and go to university.'

FARIDA: 'The *moudjahidates* did not work for the benefit of women after the independence. Today, some of them are in women's associations, but there are not many of us. They have left the field to the *intégrists*,[32] who are a real danger to the women.'

Analysis and comment

IN general, it is observed that the discourses developed by Houria and Farida are far from being the epic discourses found in some men's accounts, which are always broadcast by Algerian television to commemorate special dates related to the war. They are also widely reported in the press — we heard them while conducting discussions with former *moudjahidines*.

This 'modesty or discretion' is a characteristic of the feminine militant way of speaking. Indeed, concerning militancy, J Gotoritch highlights the following differences: 'The man, prisoner of his brand image, never mentions the everyday, and constructs an epic discourse. The woman, who cares less about making an impression, makes spontaneous confessions, mixing the sublime and the thousand small everyday things, according to the rhythm of memory.'[33]

It is the everyday that structures the framework of the stories obtained. The discourse of the two women is dotted with memories of the type, 'One day, I was ...', 'Once, I found myself ...' The discourse is built around minute events, many of which had to be discarded because they are not directly related to our story. When Houria and Farida speak of the war, it is the collective events directly related to the war that are mobilized. They tend to avoid all the facts that concern them as women. The militant did have an affective and emotional life during the fighting but this life is repressed, although revealed, sometimes, at the beginning of a sentence. The extended silences, an embarrassed speech, are also indicators. At other times, it is memories that they want to repel, or, more precisely, prefer to keep to themselves: 'No, I am not going to talk about that', or when it is facts they do not want to make public: 'Do not write about this'.

It is as if they wanted to preserve the experience of war from anything that may stain it while drawing selectively from their stock of memories. In doing so, and according to their vision, During-the-war, compared to Before- and After-the-war, becomes this ideal time where they, and their companions in the struggle, are exceptional, separate beings. Therefore, for Houria and Farida, the time of the war becomes a sort of lost paradise. The psychological operation which consists of embellishing the During-the-war, through the deletion of all forms of conflicts between individuals and between groups, allows for a criticism of the After-the-war. During-the-war is established as a mythical period of harmony and fraternity between human beings.

This was the formal analysis of the discourse. Let us turn now to the thematic. When marriage was proposed to Houria, her first reaction was: 'What will my family say?' Even the people in charge of the *maquis* consulted the family of Houria before accepting her and before celebrating her marriage.

For Farida and her family, militancy was a means to assert their national and cultural identity, because they were living in France. Farida was involved in the action by her father, a militant in the FLN, as was her brother. He, however, was opposed to the 'liberty' taken by his sister — that is, Farida's frequent journeys, and her meetings with men, disturbed him. The father had to intervene to restore the paternal authority. Once the war was over, Farida could not return to the country unless she married; a single woman could not live on her own. In Algeria, her husband's father, the patriarch, commanded her life. He refused to accept this woman imposed on the family by his son, because the marriage was not conducted according to the rules. Indeed, the rules of the patriarchal system stipulate that marriage is a matter regulated by the groups, the clans, and the families and where fathers, not sons, are the decision-makers. In this instance, the son had transgressed those rules.

The independence of the country was far from signifying the end of the oppression of women, the emergence of new feminine roles and statuses. Even though Houria and Farida had experienced the war and demonstrated their bravery and sense of responsibility, the power of the father and the father-in-law continues to reign and to govern their future.

There is, however, a change in the way our interviewees see their environment. For example, Houria has achieved a new position in the family structure. 'I am respected by everybody', she says. But there is an impression that in attributing a status of great importance to their daughter, Houria's family is simply reappropriating the prestige. In other words, the logic of the family has not really changed, it has simply become more relaxed towards one of its own who brought the family social prestige through her participation in the war.

In Farida's case, one notes a critical appreciation of the social order that governs the fate of women, a will to recognize the change through her adherence to the feminine associative movement, an anger against women *moudjahidates* who either settled under the shadow of a man, or strayed into power struggles.

These struggles for power were sterile, according to Farida, since the men did not want the women in the political structures they were instituting at the time of independence. They were sterile because the *moudjahidates* were pursuing individualist and very narrow interests.

Houria's status has really changed: within her family, she is the prestigious *moudjahidat*; among her neighbours, she enjoys the greatest respect. A change can also be noticed when listening to the projects formulated by Houria for her daughters: 'My daughters are free, they travel, they study ... I do not want them to live like the women of the past.'

Houria feels deep anger when talking about the actual situation of women: 'I hate colonialism and the Algerian women are colonized. I am ready to re-start the struggle to bring an end to this situation.'

On the material side, the independence meant an undeniable social promotion for Houria and Farida. Houria lives in a beautiful house in the capital; she receives a retirement pension and a pension as a former *moudjahidat*.

Farida married a high-ranking civil servant and is part of what might be called the privileged circles of the capital. These are facts that we noted but which were not evoked by our interviewees. The material dimension and the social promotion are not themes that marked their discourse. When Houria touched upon this subject, she was brief — she feels wronged: 'I have worked hard to bring up my children, I gained nothing.'

The militancy experienced by Houria and Farida was not animated by the cause of feminine emancipation. Houria was motivated by a sensation of suffocation, of being fed-up, her mother's authoritarian attitude, the misery, the exactions of the French — all these lay at the root of her involvement in the war.

Farida's father and brother were FLN militants, the family house was a refuge, so it was normal that she participated.

For both women, the lack of any political training when they became involved in the war, and even after independence, has prevented them from analysing and understanding the position of women during and after the war.

The major motivation was to get the French out. Both women are, of course, conscious of their role during the war, but without considering themselves as heroines in their country's history. As we have already noted, one detects an idealization of the period During-the-war; it was after independence that things went wrong. In fact, they are idealizing the inter-personal relationships. Thus, what makes the war good was the fact that people showed exceptional qualities. In Houria and Farida's perception of the war, the people were not mobilized around an ideology, or a precise political object. The sole objective was the ousting of the French.

Today, they feel greatly deceived and very angry, and wish, a little confusedly, to see things change. But the implication of their feelings is not evident since they say: 'Everyone [referring to the *moudjahidates*] is running after their subsistence ... it is not as before any more, the people have become selfish.' We have seen that, for Houria, Before-the-war corresponds to a period when it was impossible to live, while During-the-war was an ideal period. But when it comes to After-the-war, there is some confusion, and her vision of the world becomes less clear. The two women express very strong sentiments, including a sense of deception because women played the game of the rulers. There is a revolt against women because they accept being *colonized* (Houria's expression) by men. At the same time, they are angry since things could be different. The fate of women is unjust and, in this case, the subjects envisage the possibility of a new struggle in order to *decolonize* the women.

It must also be emphasized that the women have a negative image of women: they are not the victims of a given social order, rather they are primarily responsible for their situation. Moreover, the social structures and the political system are not considered as the primary factors determining the feminine condition. Hence, according to Houria and Farida, it is the woman who is responsible for her condition because she accepts the *humiliation*, the *colonization* (both expressions used by Houria). But, paradoxically, both women are ready to fight again to change the feminine condition.

When talking about the period After-the-war, their discourse is centred principally around the feminine question. Hence, this question, which did not concern Houria and Farida in the Before- and During-the-war phases, becomes of major significance in After-the-war.

Conclusion

THE social eclipse of women *moudjahidates* after independence is a fact. Houria, Farida, and many others, have withdrawn from public life. However, the *moudjahidates* have constituted the legitimacy of feminine struggles of the Algerian women after independence. They are, as founders of a certain feminine memory, the stakes in contemporary Algeria's struggles.

'We are the daughters of the *moudjahidates*', and 'We are the daughters of Hassiba Ben-Bouali', declare the militants of the feminine movement.

The *moudjahidates* are erased from another memory, another ideology: the Islamist ideology. With Islamism, there is no reconstruction of history in which the *moudjahidates* — and other women who made the history of Algeria, the *Kahina* for instance [34] — will be included. The feminine history, according to the Islamist vision, starts and finishes with the wives of the Prophet, Mohammed. They are the only admissible feminine model.[35] If, at the conscious level, the *moudjahidates* did not enter the war in order to shake the patriarchal system, or to promote feminine emancipation, and if the FLN did not worry about the feminine question, it remains that the presence of women in the war for national liberation was the premise for future feminine struggles. Hence, the *moudjahidates* are the reference for the women taking part today in a modern project of feminine liberation, in opposition to the project of the Islamist movement. [36]

N Saadi notes: 'It is through the participation of women in the creation of a modern state, born out of the war, that the feminine question is a major political question, in the sense of a city affair that calls the attention of the governors and all the actors in the political scene.' [37]

Finally, the accounts of Houria and Farida are to be situated in the *après-coup*, as mentioned earlier — that is, reordered memory. Similarly, the questions to the *moudjahidates* (Houria and Farida), those whom we asked and those we would have liked to ask, are also to be understood in the context of the preoccupations and interests of the women of today. In other words, when we speak to the *moudjahidates* of the war and then tackle the feminine question, we ask questions that are specific to the present period. Thus, we transpose to the past a question that emerged in the social field after independence.

It is the expectations, the aspirations and the ties established with the recent past through the women's participation in the war that makes the *moudjahidates* the mothers of the contemporary women's struggle.

Notes

1. War or revolution? The use of one or the other term is a function of the appreciation of the movement started in 1954. For some, it is a war for national liberation — which is our view — for others, it is a revolution.

2. Hocine Ait Ahmed, *Memoires d'un combattant* (Paris, 1983); Yacef Saadi, *Souvenir de la Bataille d'Alger* (Paris: Julliard, 1962).

3. In particular: Mohamed Harbi, *Le FLN, Mirage et Realité*, in *Jeune Afrique*, 1980, and Mustapha Lachraf, *L'Algerie, Nation et Societé* (Paris: Maspero, 1965).

4. *Moudjahidines* (m), *Moudjahidates* (f): fighters, combatants.

5. *Maquis*: a location in terrain to which access is difficult (generally in mountains with dense vegetation) where the *moudjahidines* and, in general, armed resistance groups used to gather.

6. *Fidaiyates*: militants responsible for the urban guerrilla.

7. The Battle of Algiers: The National Liberation Front (FLN) and the National Liberation Army (ALN) took the war to the capital. Women played a major role in the urban guerrillas. The French reacted violently, executing and arresting hundreds of Algerians and surrounding districts inhabited by Algerians, particularly the Casbah.

8. 'To put on the apron' means to become a cleaner, housekeeping for other people.

9. Fatma is a first name of many Algerian women. The *colons* called all the women cleaners Fatma. Stripping an individual of his/her name is a form of depersonalization.

10. *Le Vent des Aures* tells the story of a mother whose son was arrested by the French army. She did not know where he was being detained. The film shows her wandering through detention camps in many towns and cities, looking for the son, guided only by information about concentration camps gathered from all possible sources. She did not speak the language of the colonizer; all she possessed was two chickens that she intended to offer the camp wardens in exchange for information about her son.

11. The three Djamila were distinguished *fidayates* during the Battle of Algiers. In common with most women who took part in the war, they were very young. They operated alongside Yacef Saadi, the commander of the armed resistance in Algiers. All three were arrested and tortured by the French army. Djamila Bouhired was arrested in April 1957, Djamila Bouazza was arrested in May of the same year. They were the first women to be given capital punishment. Hassiba Ben-Bouali was eighteen when she joined the FLN in 1956 as part of Yacef Saadi's network. When the French army started looking for her, she took refuge in a house in the Casbah. She died on 8 May 1957 when French paratroopers blew up the house.

12. The exact French word in the original paper is *idéel*, from *idée*, (idea).

13. The two selected for this study are referred to as Houria and Farida, both members of the National Organization of Former Moudjahidines, with proven war records.

14. Frantz Fanon, *Sociologie d'une Revolution* (Paris: Maspero, 1982) (first published in 1959).

15. From now on, the quotes indicate the accounts of Houria and Farida.

16. The eight-day strike was initiated by the FLN in 1956. It was to mobilize all Algerians to show their attachment to the FLN and hence to the idea of independence.

17. She says later on that the women were afraid of being raped.

18. 'Going to the *djebel*' meant joining the war.

19. *Moussabel:* an FLN militant operating in the city.

20. *Djounouds*: soldiers of the ALN.

21.' Si' is a term signifying respect to the named person.

22. 'Brothers' is a term used for combatants. Women were called 'sisters'.

23. Mohamed Harbi, cited by Djamila Amrane (p. 250), said: 'The girls who wanted equality with men had many difficulties. It was considered that their behaviour, their desire for equality was an indication of easy morals. This is why in 1957-58, the majority of women were transferred outside the country.' Djamila Amrane does not seem to agree with this thesis. Her opinion is that 'given the unavailability of the archives of the FLN-ALN, it is impossible today to analyse and define the reasons for such a decision'. However, two facts must be emphasized: a) the affirmation of M Harbi concerning the transfer of women to Tunisia, confirms Houria's discourse. b) This question has never been addressed in debates on women's participation in the war. While completing this chapter, we learnt of the publication of a book by a former *moudjahida*, Djamila Amrane, *Les Femmes Algériennes dans la Guerre* (Paris: Plon, 1991). This book is proof that the *moudjahidates* can regain their voice. As far as we are concerned, the reading of this book allowed us to enrich our reflection.

24. *Kachabia* is a sort of very large and loose coat.

25. Operation Challes: an operation that consisted of isolating the FLN from its external bases through a policy of mass deportation from 1959.

26. *Chouhada*: martyrs, or the men who died in the war.

27. She later told us that she was a woman of easy morals.

28. Before the adoption of the Family Code, there was a judicial code concerning private men-women relations. The judges' decisions were often based on local customs. In the case of Houria, the divorce was granted by mutual consent.

29. *El baraka*: a belief investing beneficial powers in a person, or her clothes in this case.

30. For Houria, nothing is worse than colonialism. She uses the term colonized, to describe the state of oppression of the women.

31. *Front Islamiqe du Salut*, or Islamic Salvation Front: political party of religious obedience.

32. *Intégristes*: fundamentalists, or members of FIS.

33. Cited by Djamila Amrane in *Les Femmes Algériennes dans la Guerre*, p. 279, see note 23.

34. Kahina: Her real name was Dihya. She was the leader of the federation of tribes of all North Africa, until her death. At the head of her army, she opposed the invasion of North Africa by the Arabs who called her Kahina, or female prophet (Kateb Yacine,

Alger Republicain, No. 9, December 1989). In the collective memory, she is remembered under this name as a political and a war leader.

35. For an elaboration, see C Bouatta and D Cherifati-Merabtine, 'The Social Representation of Women in Algeria's Islamist Movement', in V M Moghadam (ed.) *Identity Politics and Women: Cultural Reassertions and Feminisms in International Perspective* (Boulder, Colo: Westview Press, 1994).

36. C Bouatta, 'Feminine Identity and Nationalism', forthcoming.

37. N Saadi, *La Femme et la Loi en Algérie* (Alger: Bouchène, 1991).

Translated from the French by A Bensouiah.

Chapter 3

Algeria at a crossroads: national liberation, Islamization and women

Doria Cherifati-Merabtine

IN the history of contemporary Algeria, the War of National Liberation constitutes a fundamental point of reference in the anti-colonial struggle. It was a moment of radical breakdown with no political solution. Its revolutionary character lies in the fact that it engaged the whole of society. Its popular character was the source of important initiatives and influenced the course of the war. It was also very different from previous forms of uprisings, such as those led by tribal hierarchies. These features continue to establish the movement's historical and popular legitimacy, both at home and abroad. The Algerian armed struggle became a model within the global movement of national liberation.

The liberation struggle began on 1 November 1954, under the leadership of the National Liberation Front (FLN), and entailed enormous suffering for Algerians. Each Algerian bears in his or her mind the indelible imprint of the crimes, tortures, and humiliations endured during these seven and a half years of struggle for national liberation. As for women, they remind us of the great feats and of the fighters' courage through their songs in the epic mode. Immortalizing the heroes in our recollections, they are, once again, an invaluable social memory of all peoples. In this sense, the war is told by women. This way of speaking makes women emerge from the bottom of their cells. In a bruised poetry, they reveal a daily life and a certain outlook on war. In this expression by women, it is a troubled world that emerges; it indicates the rise of a New Algeria. Did this war, which women survived, change society's opinion regarding women?

This question is important in that women's participation in the War of National Liberation was a mass event that added to the revolutionary character of this war. Moreover, this phenomenon aroused great admiration on the part of many observers and was taken as an example within the global movement of national liberation. With independence, the decline that society brought about in its relationship with women, and the disappearance of the heroines — who had given the War of Liberation its hours of glory — from the political and public scene do raise problems for those who are listening to an Algeria trying to construct itself. Does this aspect mean that the political power simply made use of women in this war and that, in fact, the revolutionary process was built without taking into consideration the position of women and without considering women as subjects and agents of history?

The answer to this question might have been straightforward, but it has been complicated by the emergence of a social fact: Islamism.[1] Indeed, the Islamist movement, which concerns Algerian society as a whole, seems to abandon any reference to the War of National Liberation and of its symbols. Islamism tends to demolish the model of the *moudjahidat*, setting up in opposition to it women's figures who conform to the Islamic projection of society. We shall presently examine the relationship between politics and women's representation from a 'representational' point of view.

This is why we shall examine the social and symbolic status of women during the colonial era and the War of Liberation. What are the dominant representations as regards the status of women? What is the relationship between this 'representational' universe and the political domains? Indeed, the emergence of the heroine as a positive female figure is built on real facts: those of the *fidayates* (militants responsible for the urban guerrillas), *djoundiyates* (soldiers of the Algerian National Liberation army [ALN]), and *moussabilates* (urban-based FLN militants). At a socio-psychological level, they are to contribute to the construction of a new woman's model, the *moudjahidat*. It is a new image which arises from and for the purpose of war. It is, therefore, unquestionable and tends to guide all the new social behaviours necessitated by the armed struggle. Its function is to minimize the clashes that could interfere between the woman's traditional image born indoors for the needs of private space and that of the *moudjahidat* born in the public space.

We shall point out that our psychological interest concerns the social representations of the fighting woman and particularly the representation of the heroine, the enlightened image of women's behaviour. The socio-historical aspects we are treating contribute, in this context, to a better understanding of past and present representations, rather than to the expression of social facts reconstructed by historians.

The Algerian woman during the colonial era

THE anti-colonial struggle engaged millions of women. Algeria was part of this dynamic and enabled Algerian women to emerge from the bottom of a society which had confined them in a traditional role. This confinement expressed, to an extent, the will of a society that was deprived of everything and wanted to survive. Its structures destroyed, deposed from its land, obliged to migrate to towns and cities, submitted to starvation and epidemics, society took refuge in tradition and custom. In trying to cut off women from Western civilization it tended to preserve itself from the West.

In this function of biological and symbolic reproduction assumed by women, it is the whole community's survival which is perpetuated. It is on women's side that one can find the identity of these deprived people. To this end, the Islamic order is jealously preserved in a spatial dichotomy that perpetuates the role of division — private space is relegated to the sacred whereas public space is considered illicit for women. These two spaces are mutually exclusive. They channel different — if not conflicting — realities.

In this division, a representation of women's social functions is being built that chooses the family as refuge and a haven of values. In this perspective, the woman becomes 'the guardian of the Algerian homeland formed to entrench traditional values in opposition to foreigners' influences'.[2]

Colonial fantasy

THE Western world, in our case France, took over the country 'by right of war', and in so doing realized its dream, charged with exoticism. The East became its dream world, its fantasy, but also its mirage.[3] The Muslim woman, invisible to the Westerner, haunted his imagination. As she was impenetrable and also impossible to possess, she was, at first, presented as a mythical and highly eroticized image. Mathéa Gaudry's description of the Eurasian is a good example of this:

Both *azriya* and *Kahina*, courtesan and sorceress, strong due to the power conferred by this dual quality, united to religion due to profound roots, it appears that she responds to the need of mysticism and wonders which occupy the ancient Berber soul ... she is like the incarnation of a collective and secular dream.[4]

In this colonial mental universe, woman is rapidly transformed from a fantasy and dreamlike image into an outdated instrumentalized object, to inhabit a world raised to a status of refuge, the family. She, then, embodies backwardness. Colonel De Lartique's remarks on this subject are explicit:

What they want to do to men, they do through women. Among civilized people, and even more so among primitive people, it is always by working on the female spirit that they invade the family ...[5]

Thus, from an erotic image, woman becomes a symbol of backwardness. She never at any time exists for herself. She is only a vector of penetration of a subjective universe that is still unknown and looks more and more like a citadel of resistance. Therefore, it is thanks to women that the Muslim community can preserve its lost identity. The perpetuation of the patriarchal order, which sets women and family in a relationship totally cut off from history, adds to this determination to survive.

Women's socio-economic reality on the eve of the war

IN this colonized world women lived confined to a family space that was marked by the colonial fact. They suffered from the hard realities of illiteracy and unemployment. The capitalist society which had penetrated their world by violence had reduced them to the status of day worker or unemployed workers' wives. In rural areas, those women whose husbands had emigrated exchanged their labour to feed their families. Songs and adages bear witness to the life of these women who were obliged to weave as well as to work in the fields. City dwellers had long since learnt to endure poverty with dignity, and demonstrated a great capacity for coping with destitution. They embroidered, sewed and devoted their time to menial activities at home that ensured a minimal financial return; this helped them to face some of the problems of life.

Constrained by sad circumstances, such as the death of a husband, a minority would set out to challenge the 'wage citadels'. In 1954, statistics indicate that there were 37,717 Muslim working women and that most of them were domestic housekeepers. Soon, it appeared that their only means of earning a salary was to sell their woman's skill. Another group of wage-earners — essentially apprentices, female workers, packers and unskilled workers — has been estimated at 7,165. In certain regions, like Tlemcen, they were called the *bent el fabrica*, or 'the factory girls'. But to the Muslim eye, the factory, which was no more than a workshop, was regarded as a lost place. The difficulties that beset these women, who needed to work in people's homes and in factories, led Mohammed Dib to say that 'the seclusion of Muslim women is a myth'. He recounts their great subjective intensity and the heartbreak endured by the women who were obliged to work. Moreover, they were battling with two worlds, the cramped and poor Muslim districts, and luxurious and comfortable European suburbs. The first world denied her because she had transgressed the forbidden; the second denied her identity and integrity in so far as it had placed her in a non-world. Her endurance and her identity, which were cracking under life's pressures, epitomized the unbearable and unmanageable aspects of this Muslim community. This endurance expressed itself in the political struggles and in the relationship that politics bears to society, culture and, therefore, to this 'representational' universe constructed around tradition that had made women differ from the other — the Western world.

Women and the modern national movement

THE development of a modern national movement, influenced both by the philosophy of the Enlightenment and by the ideas of the Nahda movement in Egypt, helped to change society's outlook on women.[6] In the dynamics of the anti-colonial struggle, a new approach to the family and to women's status imposed itself on the national liberation militants in search of a synthesis between change and stability.[7]

It is worth recalling that, in the political and social context of that time, the approach to the position of women was very sensitive. How did the political parties behave regarding women's status in society? The religious movement of the *ulama* led by Sheikh Ben Badis chose a cautious solution but this does not mean that it never had to express itself on this question. At this time, there was deep resistance towards any attempt to improve women's social status, even in the bilingual, educated milieux. As A Mérad writes:

> One small detail will provide an idea of the extreme reticence of Muslim circles in respect to women's questions during the 1930s. At the congress organized by Muslim teachers in Tlemcen, there were shouts and grumbles in the hall when attempts were made to raise the issue of the emancipation of Muslim women.[8]

This attitude reveals the difficulty of speaking about this problem but also reveals that things were beginning to change.

It is not a coincidence that the issue was raised in the circle of teachers. This liberating vision was mixed with political and individual aspirations. For the national liberation militants, and above all for the young teachers, it expressed a desire to take a wife who would become a companion even if Monique Gadant remarks that this image of a new ideal woman is that of a woman dreamt by a man, moulded by him and in his own image. Gadant also points out, however, that in this educated milieu 'the break with the patriarchal family model is a part of the ideology'.[9]

In the 1940s, the evolution of the national question showed itself in the integration of women in political parties. The creation of two women's organizations revealed the same need: for intensified action by women in support of the actions of political parties. The Algerian Women's Union (UFA) was created in 1943. It was initiated by the Algerian Communist Party (PCA) which clearly pronounced in favour of equality between the sexes. But, it saw the realization of this aim in women's capacity to participate in the transformation of society by the side of the working class. The UFA was composed mainly of Europeans but this did not prevent Muslim women from assuming leading positions, including Abassia Fodil who was to be assassinated by the OAS in the Oran region.[10] Similarly, we find the names of militants in this organization involved in the armed struggle underground network. Among them was Lucette Laribère, who was involved in underground liaison work by the side of Bachir Hadj Ali.[11] Other Communist Party and UFA militants joined the *maquis*; one such was Raymonde Peschard, who was killed in action.[12]

In 1947, the Association of Algeria's Muslim Women (l'AFMA) was created in the wake of the MTLD-PPA.[13] This association directed its efforts towards the development of women's solidarity with the political detainees, who were imprisoned after the harsh repression that followed the 8 May 1945 nationalist demonstrations. This action concerned the detainees' families.

Under the cover of charitable activities, political actions adapted to women's requirements began to emerge. The independence issue spread among women. The names of two women attracted attention in this association: Mamia Chentouf, who was a midwife, and Dr Nefissa Hamoud. When the armed struggle began, the former joined the FLN, while the latter was attracted to the *maquis*. They were the most well-known among the activists, but there were many others, like Fatema Ben Osmane, who set up the first women's cell in Tlemcen. These associations participated in the mobilization of women. Flexible forms of action and organization adapted to Algerian society allowed women to gravitate into politics. But, while UFA leaders were members of the Central Committee of the Communist Party, AFMA members did not assume leading positions in their organization. Consequently, the creation of women's associations constituted a first stage in women's entry into the contemporary political arena.

These slow but nevertheless important advances were carried on against a backdrop of the nationalist parties' campaign on women's right to vote. But there were also quarrels, like those between the MTLD-PPA and the Algerian Communist Party, concerning the problem of women's work. The former opposed women working outside the home because it was determined to find an alternative solution to the chronic unemployment of men in the Muslim community. In turn, the PCA, whose female members were mostly salaried employees, disputed this approach. These hesitations and controversies were probably due to the fact that 'revolutionary nationalism would go the way of the *Ulema* ... enclosing the woman in the sacred and the timeless'.[14]

Politics in its modern meaning expressed, therefore, an ambivalence towards women's social status. However, despite real resistance, women's names began to emerge in this men's world; these were the militants who belonged to political parties. The fact that they were leaders of women's associations does not categorize them as feminist militants, concerned solely with claims specific to women: these women emerged out of the social cause or the national question. Clearly, their status as educated women facilitated an understanding of their objectives. However, it is their quality as militants of a cause broader than their own specific women's cause that earns the recognition of Muslim opinion. Conversely, if the Oulema association has no women's organization, it has classes in *medersas* (religious schools) for girls only where they are taught in Arabic. Thanks to this action, two *moudarissate* women appeared in Algiers, the sisters Chama and Khadra, who, when the armed struggle began, joined the resistance.

Women and war: from anonymity to heroism

ON 1 November 1954, the armed struggle began. This event made women emerge on to the public scene, first in small groups, then in greater numbers. Their commitment to this liberating struggle took many forms. An inquiry by Djamila Amrane into the catalogue of war veterans in 1978 indicates that of 10,949 militant women, 9,194 (84 per cent) were members of the OCFLN [15] and 1,755 (16 per cent) were in the ALN. These figures concern women who were permanently involved in the war. J Dejeux sums up Amrane's data as follows:

> The women of the OCFLN assumed the responsibility for refuge and supplies, acting as liaison agents and guides, collectors of medicines, munitions; as terrorists (2%), the most spectacular role, they were condemned to death and pardoned; of the 65 *fidayates* counted, 33 were arrested and detained and 4 were killed. Of the young women of the ALN, 51% were under 20 years of age and 95% were under 30 years of age. They were the mainstay of the infirmaries, they were laundresses and combatants, but the last appears to have been an exception. [16]

According to Amrane: 'the armed woman combatant was certainly not a reality, but rather a myth, perhaps based on a few individual cases which struck the popular imagination'. [17] They represent only two per cent of the 3,271 known cases. If the *moudjahidates* were not on the front lines, they did assume, however, very important traditional tasks at the expense of their life.

Teguia points out that:

> In certain regions, the example of the presence of urban female militants in the FLN and the ALN induced the peasants to admit that women could also make a contribution to the struggle, and when this principle was admitted, peasants participated enthusiastically. Their [the women's] cloistering was lifted when they received the support of the ALN. [18]

The construction of the Moudjahidat symbol

Legitimation of the illicit: In the towns, the war propelled women into the streets, which consequently became a conquered place. These women transformed their appearance for the purpose of the struggle by increasingly adopting Western woman's appearance. The newness of this situation lay in the fact that, as Fanon puts it:

> One must constantly bear in mind the fact that the active Algerian woman instinctively learns her role of a woman alone in the street and in her revolutionary mission. It is in this learning process, without a rehearsal, that she goes out onto the street, three grenades in her handbag or the report of the battle zone activities in her bodice ...[19]

For women who went out unveiled for the purpose of the struggle, unveiling was not based on a principle that rested on a revolutionary doctrine.[20] That is why this gesture, which did not engender any ideological discrepancy in the active period of resistance, was more like an expression of a sacred ritual than a political stand.[21] This act has nothing to do with 13 May 1958 when, on Mrs Massu's initiative, Muslim women took off their veils on Algiers' Forum Square. No confusion exists between this attitude and that of the militant. It bears no resemblance to the so-called 'liberating' gesture of the French colonizer embodied by 'the paramilitaries and the Europeans who laughingly tear off women's veils'.[22]

This woman took off her veil for the purpose of struggle, not to look like 'a woman liberated by the soliders of pacification'.[23] If the latter was alienated, the young *fiday* was a woman who entered the scene of history. She did not owe her emancipation to the colonizer; she owed it to her commitment. Thus, the FLN's central organ, *El Moudjahid*, preferred the term 'Muslim woman', which, in this context, had a political rather than religious connotation, to 'liberated woman'. This woman became an individual thanks to the perilous mission she had chosen, which led her to suffer imprisonment and repression. For this group of militants, this double reality diminished the significance of the veil when it became an element of differentiation, opposition, and struggle for the great majority of women. The veil became a symbol. Its *ritualization* divested the militants of anonymity. They became subjects of history.

Women's acts of war: In this long war, women's exploits were commented on by newspapers with either approval or condemnation, depending on the cases. Thanks to their acts, these women became prominent figures in this troubled period. They were the heroines of the War of Liberation, some of whom have an international reputation. Among them, for example, were Djamila Bouhired, the first woman to be sentenced to death; Djamila Bouazza, Jacqueline Guerroudj, Zahia Khalfallah, Baya Hocine and Djoher Akrour, who were sentenced to death by a juvenile court. Hocine and Akrour were only sixteen years old when they were condemned to death. The lives of all these women were saved thanks to the pressure of international opinion.

Other women were the subject of commentary. There were the cases of Hassiba Ben Bouali, aged twenty, killed in the Algiers Casbah; Yamina Abed, wounded, had both her legs amputated at the age of twenty; Djamila Boupacha was known to have endured appalling torture before being imprisoned; Djennet Hamidou was killed, aged seventeen, as she tried to escape. [24]

The exploits of militants who managed to escape from La Roquette prison made their impact on popular imagery. The testimony of an imprisoned militant woman, recorded underground at the height of the war and subsequently published by *El-Hourya,* gives an account of women's life in Serkadji prison quarters:

> At the end of 1956 and the beginning of 1957, the women's quarter of Barberousse held only a few political prisoners treated under communal law, among whom were the three nurses arrested in the *maquis* — Nadia, Houria, and Nasséra — then Jacqueline Guerroudj, Baia Hocine and Djoher Akrour. Now the arrests multiply, the prison is filled. The years 1956-58 are particularly hard. In our dormitory we are forced to put our mats out in the corridors. The dormitory is damp and cold.

In this prison, women arrived with scars and marks of torture. The same witness described them as follows:

> The new ones are pale and look exhausted. They tell us all that they have endured. All had been tortured, even the older women. They still have the signs: scabs left by electricity on the hands, feet and thighs, scars left by handcuffs on the ankles, swollen hands, infected wounds ...

Torture was, in this world of war, an institution. Many militant women and men who survived retained physical as well as psychological after-effects.

Historical background of the women's national struggle

NO women occupied a leadership position in the national struggle,[26] revealing the absence of a woman's project. Although women's mobilization, and their active support of the armed struggle, was a historical necessity, this did not result from a clear political stand regarding the women's issue. Indeed, at no time did women appear in the FLN discourse as a group who had made a claim concerning their status, on which a political position was required to be taken. In debates on the projects of society there was no specific commitment regarding women.

The Soummam Charter, for example, glorifies 'the exalted revolutionary courage of the girls and women, the wives and the mothers, of our sister *moudjahidates,* who actively participated and, occasionally with weapons in their hands, sacrificed themselves in the struggle for the liberation of the homeland'.[27]

The young girls adopted an attitude that accorded with this judgement. They refused to marry men who were not involved in the struggle, invoking the fighter women at the beginning of the colonial era. It was an expression of resistance, a refusal of a union which would turn its back on Algeria's honour. This gesture symbolized Woman-Algeria that resisted the enemy and the colonizer. *El-Hourya* , for example, considered the women's demonstrations of 11 December 1960 an expression of 'the heritage of a grand tradition of struggle'.[28] In glorifying women, a link was made between their past and present struggles; the courageous acts of some women's groups and the names of chief warriors were recalled. War favours a reappropriation of women's resistance history.

A new image of woman

THE modern construction of the image of the militant woman thus takes root in history. There is a kind of metaphorization of the code of honour. Generally, women at the beginning of the colonial era supported men. Their logistic and moral support was nourished as the source of the tribe's honour, of which men were the vigilant guards. This is why the following image appears in many writings:

> Algeria-Woman is Algeria which does not want to fall into the hands of the enemies so as not to be reduced to slavery and subjugation, which does not want to be possessed by others ... (and) would rather be dead than be possessed by others. Finished are beautiful words and love songs; if you are men, the women cry to their own, show it on the land, in battle. If you have red blood in your veins, prove it, don't recoil.[29]

The emergence of this image confers a sense of history on women's contemporary struggle. War engenders a conceptualization of society that sometimes has socialist tendencies. This preoccupation may be accompanied by a new outlook on woman's status. *El-Moudjahid*, in fact, manifests an attitude of ambivalence between women's traditional status and a 'new modern status, created if not developed and valued by war'.[30]

In this insurrectionary period, therefore, the traditional image of woman began to disintegrate. For the first time, there emerged an image of modern woman, appraised and legitimated historically. This representation of the new woman was created (or developed) in non-conflictual terms *vis-à-vis* the representation of the traditional woman. This construction was based on real facts, characterizing the heroines' courage. The transformation concerning woman's representation did not entail any dissonance. It claimed to be purified of any contradiction and conflict. This new image built itself in opposition to the colonizer. This hostility established, in its turn, its own identity.

Indeed, there is here a process of anchoring, [31] that tends to perceive new women's figures as integrated with, and built up on, representations that preceded the war heroines' appearance. The return to the history of women's resistance is an example.

Post-war years

ALGERIA celebrated its independence with a great fanfare, despite the real difficulties of reconstruction. Thousands of mostly young men and women committed themselves in this new struggle without self-interest. Many people had been killed in the war; villages had been destroyed; forests burnt with napalm; there were orphaned children; and it was necessary to reconvert the economy. War widows were the first to suffer; most were obliged to look for a job. These destitute women had no other option but to become domestic servants; for them, this was the first paradox of independent Algeria. These women, who had supported their husbands or sons (who were now martyrs) and ensured the war supplies, were obliged, without any transition, to earn their living in order to feed their family. Although they received compensation from the Algerian government, this was insufficient for family needs. Thus, social self-identity acquired in time of war was followed by a depreciation in status engendered by their salaried work. However, some political measures introduced real changes in woman's status. Algeria witnessed a real revolution in education, which would have a great influence on the qualifications of salaried women, even if they remained a minority group.[32]

At the ideological level, from the beginning of 1962 we witnessed 'an ideological construction which was as much the work of the FLN as the PCA, and of the heroines of the war. This permitted a justification of women's departure from the domestic sphere with something commendable: their participation in the war, and in development'.[33] This attitude was hampered, however, when it became necessary to legislate on women's status within the family. The legislator was faced with two antagonistic representations of women: the first based on tradition, the second on modernity. This contradiction led eventually to a Family Code that established women's secular tasks and set man-woman relationships in a patriarchal mode.[34] The constitution, on the other hand, established civil rights for women. This contradiction was complicated by the advent of an Islamic trend which proposed a uniformity of views predicated on the *Sharia*. This unique source of law governs both the private and the public domains.

Faced with a national modern trend, the state was still unable to take a stand concerning women's social status. During the 1980s, in the context of this uncertainty, a contesting women's movement developed that was composed of intellectuals and working women. This movement became part of history, thanks to its specific struggles and to its meeting with the *moudjahidates* who, after a long absence, reappeared on the public scene with the struggles over the Family Code. In this context, these *moudjahidates* emerged as a group which embodied the woman's projection of society. Therefore, it is *a posteriori* that a feminine social identity, which claims to have its roots in modernity, is being constructed. The modernist women's movement chose this moment to appropriate female martyrs of the war of liberation, outside the FLN, and also those belonging to the national resistance movement. Names of famous women fighters such as Fadhma N'Soumer are associated with this contesting movement. The discourse, which legitimates women's participation in the War of Liberation, contributes to establishing the legitimacy of the project.

But when the modernist women's movement situated itself in a national history, other women who claimed to belong to the Islamist current, turned aside from this approach and all its models. Women favoured by the Islamist current are those who marked the advent of Islam. This representation of women is in accordance with the Islamic projection of society. Contemporary models with which girls identify are those of the women proselytisers, the *daiates*, represented, for example, by the Egyptian Zayneb El-Ghazali. The Afghan *moudjahidat* overshadows the Algerian *moudjahidat*. She is praised and her *jihad* is in line with a projection that aims to establish an Islamic society, and is similar to the *Umma Islamiya*. This idea is expressed in the words of some young Islamist students in *En-Naba* newspaper:[35] 'No Mohammedan female model exists except in the model of the Afghan *moudjahidat*, who is synonymous with the most marvellous and noble cause.' This woman is a dominant model in all the meetings and exhibitions on the fighting woman.

There are other examples of the great importance of this Afghan woman. In issue number 18, the same newspaper published an Afghan woman's letter addressed to her Algerian sister, that is, her 'sister in Islam'. She describes her present task: 'I am your sister in God, I work in a modest school where I teach theology, religious education, civics, sewing and the Quran to the refugee girls in a Pakistan camp.' In fact, the letter is an appeal to solidarity. The Muslim Algerian appears as a reliable ally: the combat that unites them is the Islamic combat.

The delegitimatization of the heroine

BY contrast, the heroine of the National War of Liberation came to be depreciated. This depreciation is not overt, however. Indeed, the *moudjahidat* demystification operates by a negative appreciation of the modernist women's movement. This psychological process has a twofold function:

1. To weaken the *moudjahidat* politically. At the same time, she is associated with 'the hawks of neo-colonialism'. This qualification was attributed to women who demonstrated in front of the Prime Ministry in order to denounce the attacks directed against women after the anti-women campaign led by Islamic movements, more precisely by the Islamic Front of Salvation (FIS). Another leader, who claims to belong to a more moderate stream, compared the demonstrations of the women's democratic movement to those of 13 May 1958 when Muslim women took off their veil publicly.

2. To delegitimate the *moudjahidat* deeds. Islam gave women their rights; therefore, rights claimed by women today are those of the doomed Western world. The causes that, in time of war, legitimated the transformation from a traditional to a modern status now belong to the domain of the illicit.

The Islamists occlude the facts and principles that moulded the image of the *moudjahidat*. This deconstruction is only one aspect of a more general process that tends to legitimate the historical importance of the war of national liberation. Thus, without attacking the *moudjahidat* directly, the Islamic current compares the *moudjahidat* to the modernist associative movement and presents her as an anti-model. Similarly, the Islamic current is in a phase where it needs to reconstruct new positive referential female figures. The latter are strongly opposed to the Other-woman, that is the woman who does not conform to the Islamic Revolution. The Islamic discourse offers, therefore, an opportunity to accept women who conform to the Islamic model and to reject those who turn away from this model. It focuses on a moralizing negative interpretation of the claims of the female modernist movement to which all the social dysfunctions are imputed.

Clearly, the *moudjahidates*, the war heroines, are a reference point and an identity stake. This crystallization of the female referential models which each current carries contributes to a new social anchoring to the representation of 'women'. The *moudjahidat* model and the *moudjahidat* herself have evolved. Today, this model bears a female specificity in line with the egalitarian claim and with universality. This new construction is, at present, a woman's fact. The Islamic model is a refusal of the otherness in its national and universal dimensions. It is in its genesis essentially a male fact.

These new data oblige the modern democratic movement to have a less ambiguous relationship with women. Politics must, therefore, take a clear decision on the representation of women's status. It needs to change its line of conduct which, where women are concerned, tends to make a synthesis between change and permanence. Clearly, unlike the previous periods that marked the development of the national movement and of the war of national liberation, a female project, in the course of construction, exists today. This *woman's project* constitutes the base of redefinition of power relationships in the socio-political and symbolic domains. This dimension characterizes women's condition and should be taken into consideration. This dimension is valid for the women's groups who belong to the modernist trend, at least.

What about women belonging to the Islamic trend? Does their activism within this trend contribute to setting the terms of women's emancipation, or is it set in the struggle for a global project of society which would reduce the specificity of the women's issue? As an indication, we can see what the analysis of positions *vis-à-vis* the question of the women's vote can reveal. Do the women activists of political Islam give the same meaning to this notion, with its origins in modernity, and its links to the concept of citizenship?

Women's vote: expression of citizenship or of *jihad* ?

THE public space has been largely invaded by Islamic actors. These past years, they have fairly regularly occupied the streets: Friday prayers, marches, and other spectacular ways of occupying the city. Although women were not so conspicuous during these demonstrations, they still had their form of public and mass activism.[36] In this movement, which wants to appear as a contesting movement, we find an expression of an identity assertion: that of Muslim womanhood. This dimension gives a meaning to all the other demands relating to the status of women. These positions are usually put forward by young women at college and university. This group of women, through their public activism, also occupies the space of the city which becomes a conquered place. It is there that the difference between them and the Other-woman, who is described as a 'caricature of the Western woman', is promulgated. The Islamic press is another space which regularly organizes women's expression and shows a concern for women. This space gives a message to women who believe in the new ideals of Islam; it contributes to homogenizing the woman's ideal by presenting an image of the *New Woman*, that of the 'Muslim sister'. All this shows that Islamic society constitutes the place for fulfilment of the *soi-femme* for the benefit of the Islamic *Umma*. Indeed, this ideal is lived through the experience of contradiction. It is called for by socio-political reality and by the position of the modernist women's movement. This is exemplified by a recent event relating to the women's struggle for the right to vote.

The legislation encompassing the electoral law led to the appropriation of women's votes.[37] The modernist movement of women's associations had demanded the abrogation of one article of the electoral code. This demand rests on an equal representation for both men and women; indeed, women's right to vote is an expression of the assertion of citizenship. This latter can be achieved only if women participate fully in all the affairs of the city. The electoral act as well as the presentation of women candidates bear the same meaning. This shows the degree of integration of women within their society and their actual place there.

What of women who belong to the Islamic trend? Our reading of *En-Naba* over a period of nine months shows that the women's vote was discussed. We note that if the presentation of women candidates is taboo, women's vote is a controversial subject. It is true that the act of voting and the principle of women's representation in the consultative and deliberative authorities raise problems of power. Indeed, women cannot accede to power. The act of governing and legislating belongs to men, and men only. This conception relies on a verse from the Quran and a *hadith*.[38] This reference underlies what the theologians say. Thus it is asserted that the religious law prohibits the candidature of women for the National Assembly.[39] The vote appears as a Western invention, but if it is practised by women, it is qualified by *some conditions*. It is allowed only if it is not 'a means for women to have access to power or if it does not influence a decision concerning power'. [40] In fact, this conception relies also on a representation of 'women's nature'. Women's biological and psychological characteristics make them vulnerable beings, driven by their susceptibilities. Nevertheless, we must remember that in the Islamic representation of power, there is centralization of the religious and secular powers. It is quite out of the question that the running of city affairs should fall on women. Failure to respect this line of conduct will lead to *fitna* — moral or social turmoil.

In the same newspaper (*En-Naba*), women who express themselves seem more determined to accept the vote for women, which accords with the opinion of some Muslim activists, some well-known such as Zaynab El Ghazali, a member of the Hamas Madjliss Echoura.[41] The latter explains that the absence of women candidates is the result of a free choice on the part of Muslim women activists. This attitude is due to their determination to devote their activities to the establishment of an Islamic society. Election to political office could divert them from this mission. Women's absence from formal politics becomes, in this context, synonymous with *jihad* (holy war); it is a step towards the establishment of an ideal society.

Women's right to vote is neither the expression of an egalitarian claim nor of citizenship for women. It is, in fact, a source of homogenization of the Islamic trend. Women have proved that they are not interested in occupying leading positions in this new National Assembly. However, thanks to their vote they could contribute to establishing the Islamic *dawla* — the Islamic state.

Who are these Muslim women activists?

THE foregoing argument raises some questions regarding the identity of these militants. To this end, we shall analyse the Islamic press, for it constitutes a first stage in our investigation. Our reading of *El Mounquid* showed the importance of propaganda written for women;[42] a special page is reserved for them. The target readership, which favours Islam, and readers' letters reveal a unanimity of views on questions related to women. Those who sign these letters are largely college and university women, as we find also when reading *En-Naba*.

What is expected from the Muslim activist? According to one woman leader in the Hamas Madjliss Echoura, 'the starting point of every militant action is "acceptance", "understanding", and "assimilation" of the Islamic project'. Specific qualifications are required in order to be able to accept, assimilate, and wholly understand this project. Because these Muslim activists have confidence in the Hamas movement, in practice and in theory they can be convinced easily. However, if support for the moral and political line is a precondition for participation in the activities, it is not synonymous with militant actions in the party. Women assert, on the contrary, that they prefer to engage in socio-educative activities — 'they visit poor families; they organize remedial classes for pupils of nine-year basic school and for final-year pupils'. Access to theology by means of reading the Quran makes their knowledge reliable and able to be transformed into a militant activity where 'consciousness raising' and education are preferred to politics.

It is the construction of the individual and of the family that are at the root of this militant line of conduct. This preference, that is once more the result of a deliberate choice, recalls the traditional role division between men and women — the running of public affairs belongs to men; educational tasks belong to women. Within this approach it is considered that women give a new meaning to their civilizing mission. Purity of the society depends on women's purity, and the assimilation of Quranic principles are conditions for the success of the future society.

El Ilm, a notion that must be redefined

THE place and role of college and university women explain that certain notions like that of *El Ilm* (science) have to be redefined. In *En-Naba,* recommendations are clearly addressed to young women.[43] In an exhibition held at Algiers University, it was recalled that the Muslim sister must study science and Islam; she must also be on her best behaviour in order to achieve the expected goal. A future woman graduate is advised: 1. Not to forget that a diploma is not sufficient — she must have good intentions as far as religion is concerned; 2. To understand and represent the Islamic doctrine by a re-reading of the Quran and by constant research; 3. To take part in all activities (exhibitions, associations, cultural clubs) that allow her to show her role as Muslim sister; 4. To participate in the construction of the *Khalifat.*[44] The paradox of this redefinition of the notion of *Ilm* lies in the fact that Islam and science cannot be conceived of separately and that the Quran contains the essence of all the scientific theories the human intellect can discover and bring to the fore. The relation to science must not lead to the renunciation of spiritual life. No noteworthy science exists except that which is accompanied by theological learning. The return to basics is, in fact, a return to the Holy Book; it is the only way which can open up the path of knowledge. We are far from a practice that favours oral tradition. What is advised here is access to knowledge by means of the written word and reading of the Quran. At the level of syntax, this reading presents a complexity of language that makes it difficult for an uneducated person to comprehend.

Women's strategies and social antagonistic logics

THE aspects mentioned above indicate that gender dynamics exist within the Islamic current. It has produced militants who feel the need to identify with their elders and with 'Mohammedan' female models. We note that, in Islam, women distinguished themselves by their knowledge and their theological learning. To a certain extent, they were the enlightened intellectuals of the society which came out of *Djahilia*. They had in common the fact that they were the Prophet's companions. These women are characterized by their knowledge or by their participation in *jihad*. Thus, while women of the modernist trend and the *moudjahidat* distinguish themselves as gendered individuals who carry a clear, modern women's projection of society, those of the Islamic stream aim, on the contrary, diminish the visibility of women and elect to merge into a projection of society based on *Sharia*.

What characterizes the women of the modernist trend is the fact that they break with a global line of conduct which denies the specificities of the women's issue. Indeed, this line of conduct has subjected women's 'liberation' to national independence and to the building of a socialist society. The great majority of activists in the modernist women's movement are older university women, who belong to the first post-war generation of intellectuals. As they hold to liberal ideas and an egalitarian view of society, they have learnt, at their expense, that no change is possible if the outlook on woman, and her place within society, does not evolve. The historical experience accumulated by the militants of both the War of Liberation and of post-independence Algeria leads them to place recognition of the 'Woman-Individual' on the agenda.

But what is the meaning of such a claim in a society where the process of individualization remains a recent and fragile phenomenon? The affirmation of the 'Woman-Individual' revives anxiety and becomes as threatening as the images of 'Women Ogresses' that haunt the Magrebian fantasy. The visibility of women disturbs the patriarchal order and weakens men's position within society. It foreshadows the reversal of roles and gives women the opportunity to accede to real and symbolic power.

Does the dichotomy (noted above) between the female models that symbolize modernity and those which reify the Islamic female ideal, imply we are dealing with two different models? We must recall that Kadidja and Aicha, both of whom were the Prophet's spouses, are — for women of the modernist trend — part of the representational system of reference. Thus, reference to modernity is not set outside the parameters of Arabic Muslim civilization.

On the other hand, we notice that women of the Islamic trend have also taken over notions which belong to the register of modernity, such as 'the right to work', 'the right to be educated'. It is then 'an identity question of modernity', which reveals a kind of 'mixed line of conduct' where both acceptance and rejection of modernity mingle.[45] The modernist model functions also at the 'representational' level from 'a conflictual mixture',[46] and combines modernist as well as traditional representations. These two modern and traditional sections of society have converged to give rise to behaviour, attitudes, and representations different from those of the traditional society; this has become a recognized social fact. Islamism, on the contrary, advocates a return to pure and authentic tradition. Do the contradictions, the reappropriations of notions, and readjustments of sense differ from traditional society? Are we now witnessing a setting up of representations from which it seems that conflicting conclusions may be drawn, but in reality work for an autonomous 'Woman-Individual' and her characterization as an active and thinking being? These new representations are far from those of the FIS leader, who asserts that 'women are procreators of men'. Or are we witnessing the setting up of social logics that are not only different but irreconcilable?

If nothing today allows us to take a stand on the future of society, we cannot ignore that, perhaps for the first time since independence, past/present representations of women and the advent of Islam have been so much the subject of identity stakes. Moreover, this dimension has never been so closely intertwined with the future of the 'Nation-State' and its symbols.

Notes

1. Islamism refers to a politico-religious phenomenon which distinguishes itself by a political activism that seeks the Islamization of society. Islamism militates in favour of a return to the sources of Islam and the tradition of the Prophet.
2. N Zerdoumi, *Enfants d'hier* (Paris: Francois Maspéro, 1982), p. 38. All translations from French by V M Moghadam.
3. M Alloula, *Le Harem Colonial* (Genève-Paris: Editions Statkine, 1981), p. 9.
4. M Gaudry, *La Femme Chaouia de L'Aurès* (Librarie Orientaliste Faul Gauthner, 1929) p. 451.
5. Ibid.
6. The Nahda or renaissance movement in Egypt refers to the modernizing project of Muhammad Ali.
7. Monique Gadant, 'Nationalité et Citoyenneté, les femmes Algériennes et leurs

droits', pp. 293-337 in *Les femmes et la modernité, Peuples méditerranéens*, No. 44-5 (July-December) 1988, p. 293.

8. A Mérad, *Le Reformisme Musulman en Algérie de 1925 à 1940* (La Haye: Mouton et Cie, 1967), pp. 316-30.

9. Gadant, op. cit., p. 299.

10. OAS (l'Organisation de l'armée sécret) was created by the *pieds noirs* (Algerian-born Frenchmen).

11. Bachir Hadj Ali was the First Secretary of the Algerian Communist Party. The Communist Party was created in 1936. It did not accept its auto-dissolution when it was underground and in view of the FLN refusal to admit it in the Front as an independent party. The two parties came to an agreement in 1956 and individual Communist militants were allowed to join the FLN.

12. *Maquis* refers to a location to which access is difficult, where *moudjahines* and armed resistance groups used to hide.

13. MTLD-PPA: Movement for the Triumph of Liberties and Democracy-Party of the Algerian People.

14. Gadant, op. cit., p. 297.

15. OCFLN: Civil Organization of the National Liberation Front.

16. See J Dejeux, *Femmes d'Algerie: Legendes, Tradition, Histoire, Littérature* (La Boîte à Documents, 1987).

17. D Amrane, ibid, p. 185.

18. M Teguia, *L'Algérie en guerre* (Alger: OPU, 1988), p. 125.

19. F Fanon, *L'an V de la Révolution Algérienne* (Paris: Maspéro, 1968).

20. Ibid, p. 27.

21. N Allami, *Voilées devoilées, être femme dans le monde Arabe* (Paris: L'Harmattan, 1988), p. 126.

22. C Benabdessadoc, 'Pour une analyse du discours sur la femme' (compiled from *El Moudjahid* 1956-62). 'Mémoire d'étude approfondie' (unpublished manuscript, Université d'Alger, 1979), p. 150.

23. *El Moudjahid*, Tome 3 (*El Moudjahid* in three volumes, Belgrade, June 1962).

24. *El-Hourya*, No. 38, p. 5.

25. *El-Hourya*, témoignage, 1 November 1961, p. 1-2.

26. M Harbi, 'Les femmes dans la Révolution Algérienne' (Les Révoltes Logiques, Paris, no. 11, Hiver 1979-80), pp. 78-93.

27. Gadant, op. cit., p. 305.

28. *El-Hourya*, No. 38, 8 March 1961.

29. Dejeux, op. cit., p. 156.

30. C Benabdessadoc, op. cit., p. 204.

31. On this concept, see D Jodelet, 'Representation Sociale: Phenomènes, Concept et

Théorie', pp. 357-78 in *Psychologie Sociale,* Serge Moscovici (ed.), Paris: PUF, 1984.

32. National statistics of 1990 indicate that only 334,000 women work out of a 5,417,000 population, owing to political and social reasons.

33. M Gadant, 'Les communistes Algériens et l'émancipation des femmes', pp. 199-228 in *Femmes et Pouvoir,* No. 48-49, (July-December) 1989, p. 201.

34. The Family Code (9 July 1984) was finally promulgated after years of procrastination. From 1965 to 1984, a series of pilot studies were undertaken; their reactionary character provoked vivid reactions in women's circles, above all in university circles.

35. *En-Naba* is a weekly newspaper of the Hamas Party (Movement for an Islamic society). This is the only party in the Islamic current to have women in its Madjliss Echaura (consultative council).

36. An example is the important demonstration of Islamist women in front of the National Assembly on 21 December 1989.

37. Refer to article 54 of the Electoral Code. This allows men to cast votes on behalf of female kin — VMM.

38. T Gaid, *Religion et Politique en Islam* (Alger: Editions Bouchène, 1991), p. 216.

39. *En-Naba*, No. 12, p. 12.

40. Ibid, No. 7, p. 14.

41. Ibid, No. 13; No. 17, p. 14. Hamas was created in June 1991. Its president is Mahfoud Nahnah. This party has a Madjliss Echoura composed of 110 members, of whom 17 are women. Hamas presents itself as a moderate alternative to the FIS.

42. C Bouatta and D Cherifati-Merabtine, 'The Social Representation of Women in Algeria's Islamist Movement', in V M Moghadam (ed.) *Identity Politics and Women*, Boulder, Colo: Westview Press, 1994).

43. *En-Naba*, No. 6, p. 9.

44. Ibid, No. 16, p. 11.

45. N Göle, *Ingénieurs islamistes étudiantes voilées en Turquie: entre le totalitarisme et l'individualisme in intellectuels islamistes* (1989).

46. D Cherifati-Merabtine, 'Les Représentations Sociales chez un groupe d'ouvrières'. Magister en Sociologie. Unpublished manuscript, Université d'Alger, 1987.

Translated from the French by Farida Madjoub. Additional translations of extracts from the French by Valentine M Mogadham.

Chapter 4

National identity, fundamentalism and the women's movement in Bangladesh

Salma Sobhan

IF identity is defined as an awareness of self, national identity would appear to imply the awareness of self within a defined national context. It could also mean the use for political purposes — for example, mobilization for votes — of groups of people who identify themselves in a particular way. Identity, however, is not merely an internal awareness of self; it also has to do with an assertion of this self to those who are perceived as being outside this self. One aspect of this assertion is obviously to gather to oneself those whom one sees as being part of the corporate identity. The perception of belonging to the 'same' can relate to any common factor; caste, class, religion, ethnicity, and gender are only the most obvious categories. However, there is not necessarily homogeneity within such groups. In this context gender is of particular interest.

It is often found that those societies which most vigorously separate themselves externally from others on any one ground are also those in which, internally, gender segregation is likely to be present. The rationale for this segregation may be that the different spheres of activity and different roles for men and women are based on biological differences and are not an assertion of relative superiority and inferiority. And historically this may well explain the origins of such differentiations. The reality is that this difference is used as a mechanism of control, usually by men over women. This is not, of course, to say that there will not be any powerful women in patriarchal societies. The powerful matriarchs in patriarchal societies are almost a stereotype. But the exercise of power and control as a surrogate or through force of personality or both is a different issue.

The focus of this chapter is religious fundamentalism and its effect on the women's movement in Bangladesh.[1] There are two manifestations of religious fundamentalism in Bangladesh — on the one hand, an orthodox or 'mainstream' fundamentalism and a sort of 'syncretic' fundamentalism on the other. There is also the issue of the politicization of religion which will need analysis. The historical origins of all three manifestations need to be traced briefly, as well as that of Bangladesh itself.

Historical background

The emergence of Bangladesh

WHILE Bangladesh itself came into existence as a sovereign independent state only in 1971, we can trace in its various historical incarnations the surfacing and submerging of different perceptions relating to its identity. As part of the unpartitioned sub-continent, the area that is now Bangladesh and was once East Pakistan was originally the eastern wing of a large province of eastern India — Bengal. Pakistan came into existence in 1947 when the British pulled out of India and the sub-continent became independent and was partitioned. The national struggle for independence from the British had originally united the sub-continent's Hindus and Muslims, but this common goal had not proved sufficient to keep the two communities together. Eventually a large section of the Muslim population in India, having struggled for autonomy within the context of an undivided India and having failed to reach agreement with the Hindu majority on this issue, had opted to form a separate state — Pakistan.

The formula for the creation of Pakistan was 'Muslim majority contiguous areas', which meant, in practice, that the state of Pakistan consisted of two wings to the east and west of India but separated by several hundred miles of another country. The two wings of Pakistan soon found, therefore, that apart from religion they shared little in common. Further, for a number of reasons the west wing of Pakistan began to acquire dominance over the east wing. As a result the disaffected inhabitants of the east wing were soon asserting their ethnic Bengali identity against the predominantly Punjabi West Pakistanis where, earlier, they had asserted their religious identity against the Bengali Hindus. Pakistan broke up in 1971 after a bloody and bitter civil war. The west wing retained the name Pakistan, the east wing became Bangladesh.

The advent of Islam in Bengal

IN the context of undivided India, Islam was a newcomer. The first Muslims came to India in the eighth century and reached Bengal in the thirteenth century. They came to a country that had already been subject to a variety of different beliefs and settlers.

In his study of religion and development in Bangladesh, Abecassis reckons that in Bengal the first cultivators came from South Asia, bringing with them not only their skills, crop cultivation and their cattle (buffalo), but also their religious beliefs which emphasized the cult of the dead and grove worship.[2] In 1000BC, when people from the Gangetic plain began to spread into Bengal bringing with them, *inter alia*, Hindu beliefs and culture, these beliefs were subsumed rather than eradicated by them. The same had happened to Buddhism nearly 1,000 years later when it reached Bengal. Abecassis quotes Ramkrishna Mukherjee: 'Buddhism contented itself with superimposing a new religion upon the existing tribal societies ... from which it did not uproot animistic practices.' Abecassis goes on to quote Maloney and others: 'Thus Brahminical Hinduism, Vajrayana Buddhism and Mahayana Buddhism from north India and Theravada Buddhism from Burma, all mingled ... under the aegis of various kingdoms, while the peasant reverence for bamboo groves and ghosts of the dead continued at the village level.' He adds: 'The world view of the people at the time of the first coming of Islam was, therefore, probably a mixture of Hindu, Buddhist and "animist" ideas and practices, the result of a continuous process of conflict and assimilation over the preceding millenia.'

Various Muslim 'conquistadores' slowly established their rule in India. At the same time the religion of the conquerors was being spread by the seafaring missionaries and *sufis* (Muslim mystics) who brought the message of Islam with them. The peculiar configuration of Pakistan into its eastern and western wings on the east and west coasts of northern India is testimony that Islam spread over India less by conquest than by conversion. The Muslim rulers brought with them an administrative system and a language, but apart from the isolated zeal of some, for most of them it was not part of the policies to convert the indigenous population.

The Islam that was preached by the *sufis* was not orthodox. It emphasized a spiritual union with God and did not require its newest adherents to jettison their traditional beliefs and practices totally. Thus, in its early days,

Islam in Bengal became part of the syncretic tradition of the area. It was only in the wake of the Islamic revivalist or reformist movements, which started in India from the sixteenth century and spread to Bengal in the eighteenth and nineteenth centuries, that the conflict between religion and custom arose for the Bengali Muslims. And this conflict has never been truly resolved.

Gunga-Jumni is the name given to a particular type of silverware in Bengal. One side of the object is gold-washed, giving a lustre to the silver and providing a pleasing contrast. The name derives from the names of two of the mighty rivers of Bengal, the Ganges and the Jamuna. Where these two converge it is said that the different confluences have identifiably different colours, hence the name of the gold-washed silver. The Muslim Bengali psyche, too, can be likened to this phenomenon, for within it Islam and custom converge and flow together like the intermingled streams of the Ganges and the Jumna. While these two streams contribute to the richness of the culture, they are also the source of an ambivalence which can, in its worst manifestations, be likened to a sort of schizophrenia. The malaise started with the reformist movements in Islam.

The Muslim reformist movement in Bengal

WHILE this was a movement to cleanse from the body politic of Islam the syncretic practices which it followed, at the same time the reformist movement in Bengal was a very strongly political movement to organize the peasantry against both the tyranny of the Hindu *zamindar* (landlord) and the British colonial power. The reformers preached a return to the pristine and austere doctrines of Islam. But while the reformers called upon people to discard those practices and superstitions they regarded as pagan, they did not feel it necessary (nor even desirable) to try to cut off the masses from their ethnic roots. Haji Shariatullah (1781 to 1840) — one of the most dynamic of these reformers — even translated the Quran into Bengali.

The reformists tied the tenets of religious reformation to confrontation with the Hindu *zamindars* whose exaction of feudal dues relating to Hindu festivals were seen as un-Islamic by the reformers and more simply as onerous by the Muslim peasantry. Confrontation with the British colonial power was also part of the reformist platform, not least because it was they who, in the interest of the regular collection of revenue had, through legislation which turned erstwhile revenue collectors into landlords, created this Zamindar class.[3]

Thus religious identity was strongly reinforced among Muslim Bengalis by a consciousness of their political identity. These two identities coexisted with — and contradicted — each other, not even fusing in the later independence movement. The momentum of the reformist movement was felt even behind the veil.

Emancipation of the Bengali Muslim women

BY the time the British had established themselves firmly in India and had begun to allow the inhabitants of the country a voice in running it, the Indian Muslims had dropped into second place in the race. This was because, after the abortive war of independence in 1857, there had been a conscious policy of discrimination against them, and also because they remained outside the mainstream education that was necessary to join the services of the Raj. Despite this marginalization, however, there was a sense of complacency about the status of Muslim women. Writers like Katherine Mayo (*Mother India*) had fostered such feelings. Whatever might have been the theoretical basis for this complacency, it had long been subsumed by reality.

The history of the emancipation of the Bengali Muslim woman is inadequately recorded, not only in accounts about the emancipation of Indian women generally but also in accounts about Bengali women.[4] Reading some of these one might well suppose that the phenomenon had bypassed Bengali Muslim women altogether. That it did not owes not a little to the pioneering work of a handful of remarkable women, only some of whose names are known, such as those of Faizzunessa Chowdhurani and Karimunessa Khan.[5] There were others whose names have not survived, such as the Muslim woman who accompanied Miss Cook, an English social worker, on her rounds to bring Muslim girls to school. Even among these women, Rokeya Sakhawat Hossain's contribution is outstanding.

Rokeya Sakhawat Hossain was born in 1890, in Rangpur, a province of north Bengal, to a middle-class Muslim family. Her father was interested in his daughter's education, and had encouraged Rokeya in her reading. She was fortunate in being married to an equally forward-looking man, Sakhawat Hossain, who not only encouraged her to read and to think for herself but also encouraged her to write. Rokeya was eventually to focus her energies on education, but she began by recounting a series of anecdotes designed among other things to highlight the absurdity to which observance of the institution of purdah was carried.[6] There was a great furore and Rokeya was, predictably, accused of being un-Islamic, of 'selling out', and, of course, of being influenced by outsiders. What was unforgivable was that all the stories she wrote were true, and drawn from life. Rokeya, however, persevered with her writing but saw very soon that it was the younger generation to whom she could most success-fully address herself. Accordingly she set herself the task of founding a school for Muslim girls.

Rokeya Sakhawat never 'came out' of purdah. Widowed young, she devoted her life to education and had a profound influence on a whole generation of women. She remains the prototype of a devout Muslim who saw clearly the dangers of obscurantism. About religion she said: 'Using religion as an excuse, men have tried to dominate women. Thus I was obliged to enter into the fray.' This statement remains valid today.

Once the mental breakthrough was made about education, Muslim women all over the sub-continent were as eager as women anywhere to avail themselves of the opportunities which were coming the way of men. What died harder were the social taboos. These, however, were rationalized, and swept away by the momentum of the independence movement only to return, unfortunately, once the game was won.

At that stage, it should be realized, both Hindus and Muslims had gone on the defensive on the issue of the status of women. The uninhibited social intercourse between British men and women gave a misleading impression about the degree to which the British woman was emancipated, while the unequal social status of Indian women reconciled liberal British consciences to their own presence in India. Consequently, the women's movement was strengthened in the wake of the national movement for independence.[7]

The politicization of Islam

THE consciousness of the vast Muslim peasantry of Bengal had originally been awakened by the reformists against the landlord or *zamindar*. This conscious-ness was now won over to the cause of political liberation from the British. The battle was fought on two fronts — not only for freedom from the British, which as time went on became a foregone conclusion, but also for freedom from Hindu domination. Muslim peasant against Hindu landlord became the basis of a mobilization that merged class and religion. Thus, during the struggle for independence from the British, much of Muslim Bengal asserted its religious identity very strongly. Part of this assertion was the acceptance by such Bengalis that their language 'belonged' to the Hindus of Bengal. Though spoken by both Muslim and Hindu Bengalis as Urdu, the vernacular of Delhi and Lucknow (the political and cultural centre of the Mughal dynasty overthrown by the British) was, of course, primarily the language of the Muslims of north India. In fact, there were pockets of Urdu-speaking Muslims all over India, even south India at Hyderabad and Mysore especially.

In the heyday of the Mughal Empire, Persian, the language of governance, had been learnt by Hindus and Muslims alike as later English was to be. Urdu (basically a mixture of Sanskrit, Arabic, Persian, and Turkish) was now seen as a survival from the days of Muslim supremacy in India and politically sponsored as the language of Indian Muslims. Greetings and salutations were consciously Muslim. This view of the language did not survive long in East Pakistan, for it soon became clear that having Urdu as the sole national language would give the west wing an advantage, as Urdu was more widely spoken there. This attitude of mind in Bengal towards the Bengali language was symptomatic of the cultural confusion.

Despite these efforts to bridge regional and linguistic dissimilarities, it was not a homogeneous movement for all. The call for an independent Muslim state, for example, was opposed by the fundamentalists on the grounds that nationalism was un-Islamic. It is not without significance that there was also a call for a united Bengal that would be a part of neither India nor Pakistan.[8]

Throughout the period between 1947 and 1971, East Pakistan was strongly pulled by its ethnic and linguistic roots. The language movement, which reached its culmination just five years after the creation of Pakistan, was the most dramatic manifestation of these forces.

The language movement

AS already seen, the euphoria following the creation of Pakistan as a state for Muslims was shortlived. The issue of economic disparity between the two wings soon became a focus of discord. A further dimension to this discord was introduced by the question of the national language of the new state. The non-Bengali leaders of the Muslim League felt that the obvious choice was Urdu.

This did not appear to be so obvious to members from the east wing of the country. Though Urdu was neither a regional language in the west nor the east, it was more widely spoken in West Pakistan. The proposition appeared to the Bengali-speaking majority population of East Pakistan as a ploy to further marginalize the Bengalis. Widespread agitation broke out after the announcement that Urdu would be the sole national language. Following an incident where police fired on a procession, resulting in the death of three people in early 1952, the government conceded the point. Bengali and Urdu became the joint national languages of Pakistan. Because of its failure to protect the rights of the Bengalis in the early years of Pakistan, the Muslim League did not survive as a party of any importance in East Pakistan and was wiped out at the polls in 1954. But the experience of the language movement highlighted the very fundamental contradictions that existed in the new state.[9]

The ethnic assertion

IT could not really be gainsaid that the West Pakistanis had more in common with the Middle East, with Iran and Afghanistan (though politically there were tensions between Pakistan and Afghanistan) than they had with East Pakistanis. Before partition there had been little connection between the two wings of Pakistan. Now all sorts of dissimilarities began to be noticed.

The use of a Sanskrit-derived script for Bengali in contrast to the Persian script used for Urdu was only one of the many instances cited of the Hindu influence in Bengal. The radio was forbidden to broadcast the songs of [the Indian poet] Tagore. It was as if the Germans were being asked to disown Goethe. Off the air the singing of Tagore songs went on. This attitude was symptomatic of a hundred others which incensed the Bengali Muslims, leading them to assert their ethnic and linguistic identity even more strongly. Women would adorn their foreheads with a *teep* — a red spot. In the rest of India this form of decoration — a vestigial remnant of the caste mark — was worn only by Hindu women. In Bengal, however, it had become acceptable for young Muslim women to wear the *teep* and — except among families settled in Bengal but not indigenous to it — many did so; it now became *de rigeur* to wear one. It was in the way that the Bengali woman comported herself that the West Pakistanis noted the most difference between themselves and their east-wing compatriots.

Outside of its modern cities Pakistan, even today, remains a largely feudal society, with tribal attitudes towards women. In the 1950s, Bengali women, with their hair loose around their shoulders, red-tikkaed, who decorated the thresholds of their houses with *alpanas*, geometric and floral designs, to mark auspicious occasions, were looked at askance by their compatriots from the west wing. Among the Bengali middle classes, young girls were taught how to sing as a matter of form; many learned classical dancing. All this was a clear indication to the West Pakistanis that East Pakistan was, *au fond*, non-Muslim. (The fact that in the west wing Muslim girls did not inherit immovable property from their fathers, which was clearly un-Islamic, occasioned no comments about non-Muslim influences, however: an excellent illustration of the mote in another's eye being more visible than the beam in one's own.)

Things came to a head in 1971 when civil war broke out between the two wings over the issue of handing over of power to the successful East Pakistani-based political party which would have effectively ended the west wing's domination at the centre.[10] The war was sold to West Pakistanis, however, not as a fratricidal war but as a *jihad*, or a holy war against the infidel. The war was fought in the east wing with a ferocity that remains inexplicable. As in all wars, women were a particular target for the soldiers who boasted that they would 'convert' East Pakistan through engendering true Muslims. The crackdown by the army was fiercely resisted both by the Bengali units of the Pakistani army which had been disarmed before the crackdown, and most notably by a popular army of guerrillas — both men and women.

All civil wars are nasty affairs, but the ideological perceptions of the west wing about the causes of the conflict, the calling into question of their Muslim faith, first amazed and then disillusioned the East Pakistanis about the solidarity of the *Umma*. The civil war became a war of national liberation and Bangladesh came into existence. East and West Pakistan went their separate ways.

The 14 years (from 1947 to 1971) of being on the defensive as Muslims, culminating in the liberation war, left many Bangladeshis feeling traumatized. Many Bangladeshis were also determined that religion should never again be a political determinant. Yet a legacy of that trauma is that the behaviour of women remains the touchstone to determine the purity of Muslim Bengal. Secularism was indeed born of the 1971 war. The question is — can the infant survive?

Bangladesh — a secular society?

IT WOULD appear that following the creation of Bangladesh in 1971, the assertion of its Muslim faith has slowly increased. The implications of this for Bangladesh as a whole, and for women in particular, need careful analysis. But though the pendulum swings between the religious and ethnic identity have a historical context within Bangladesh, this most recent swing towards religion manifests a zeal that has its origins elsewhere.

Economically, Bangladesh could not have come into existence at a worse time. The 1950s and 1960s, with their easy loans and the boom of the Korean war, were over. In the 1970s, the OPEC countries made a bid for the play. But the new players for power on the international political scene had no use for Bangladesh. The Muslim and Arab states had not supported Bangladesh in her struggle against Pakistan. The new state had not even been recognized by them in the beginning. On the other hand, India, despite having been supportive of Bangladesh during the liberation struggle, became suspect, perhaps because of her size and proximity. She was so near and so big, and look at what had happened to Kashmir, Hyderabad, Goa, Sikkim, and Bhutan. The failure of the populist government to deliver economically was another factor contributing to disillusionment with the ethnic identity. The pendulum began — if not to swing away — to rest dead centre. It was at this point that the military took over.

Militarization and fundamentalism

AN army take-over is never popular, no matter how unpopular the regime it displaces. This applied particularly in Bangladesh with memories of the atrocities of 1971 still quite fresh in the minds of most, despite the floods and famine of 1974. By 1975 Bangladesh had been recognized by the Muslim and Arab world, and had attended an Islamic summit meeting. Despite this, considerable numbers of Bangladeshis who had felt aggrieved at the lack of support from the Islamic world in 1971 still felt unhappy at the tacit questioning of their Muslim identity that this failure had implied. Thus the Islamic card was the obvious one for all succeeding governments to play. And this they did.

The governments of Bangladesh had other more material reasons for wishing to be accepted into the Islamic fold. The Middle East had become the El Dorado of South and South-East Asia, with thousands of workers going there and remittances pouring back to their own country. Economically it made sense to be a Muslim. (Though, of course, this criterion was hardly necessary *vide* the Koreans, Filipinos *et al*, who also flocked to the Middle East.) In fact, the Middle East governments were keen merely to diversify their expatriate intake and made no special concessions to co-religionists. But once Bangladeshis started going in numbers to the Middle East they felt part of the Muslim scene again, despite disillusionment over the lack of hospitality in the host country.

The original constitution of Bangladesh had enshrined secularism as one of the four basic tenets of the state. This article was now amended and the word secularism deleted. An article was added making Islam the guiding principle for the state and introduced by the words Bismillah hir-Rahman hir-Rahim.[11] A subsequent regime made Islam the state religion of Bangladesh. The stage was being set for the revival of the influence of religious parties.

The liberation movement had had its share of collaborators. Notable among this class had been the religious parties who saw the assertion of Bengali identity and language as un-Islamic. These parties now began to come into their own. The liberation war in all but words was portrayed as a conspiracy between un-Islamic forces in Bangladesh and the enemies of Islam — in this case India. (This ploy succeeded not only because people were aggrieved at having their religious credentials questioned but also perhaps because many Indian Muslims were dismayed by the break-up of Pakistan, and liberal Indians were also critical of India's role in Bangladesh's liberation struggle.)

Apart from the surfacing of organized religious parties there was a reappearance on the scene of the cult of the *pir* [Muslim sage or holy man]. The acolytes of the missionaries and *sufis* who had preached Islam and had come to be known as *pirs* had, in their turn, become *pirs* themselves, passing on the mantle from one generation to another and exercising a great influence on their followers. *Pirs* have never been part of the orthodoxy of Islam. But where the original *sufis* were mystics extolling the spirit rather than form, the *pirs* of today preach an Islam of superstition and ritual. Sufiism preached control over self as the paramount discipline. Today's *pirs* preach control over others.

We have seen how the psyche of the Muslim Bengali is already trapped between the forces of ethnicity and religion. The latter focused particularly on women. This is an historical phenomenon. The earlier age operated to deny women access to information that would keep them in touch with the world. Thus, learning Bengali was considered unnecessary for girls. The ability to read the Quran in Arabic — which, as they were taught only the script and not the language, was incomprehensible — was all the literacy deemed necessary for girls. This had been the attitude in respect of boys, but the exigencies of survival forced a change. Since women were not supposed to move outside their homes, logically they did not need to learn to read and write Bengali.

Thus, when Karimunessa picked up the Bengali alphabet by hearing her brothers repeat their letters and was allowed to go on studying by her father when he found her tracing her letters in the sand, the poor man was not only criticized for being an unfit father, but the child was sent away to her maternal grandfather's house. She was married off at 14 but her brother-in-law taught her to read. When she was widowed at an early age, this was seen as a punishment for having stepped out of her sphere. The same was later said about Rokeya Sakhawat Hossain when she was widowed young. (It is interesting to note that access to religious writing was not denied the women, which is often the prohibition in other societies and communities.)

The politics of Islam

THE last twenty years have seen Bangladesh enter a new phase. Since 1975, successive regimes have made religion part of the state machinery while acting out of pure opportunism. This has greatly strengthened the fundamentalists, who would never have had the political clout to have secularism removed from the constitution or to make Islam the state religion. These governments were able to get legislation through unrepresentative parliaments, which were tacitly backed by the military. The reassertion of the religious identity phenomenon is, of course, something which is occurring all over the world — Hinduism in India, Born-Again Christianity in the West, and Jewish fundamentalism in both the West and Middle East, as well as Islamic fundamentalism — each group drawing strength from its rivals. But the governments in Bangladesh have not been fundamentalist. They were only being opportunist but their opportunism has helped the fundamentalist cause.

The regimes that pandered to the fundamentalists also passed legislation to deal with social evils which affected women, but this was in the context of merely giving with one hand to take away with the other. One does not need to elaborate the dangers of using religion as a political weapon. It is not without significance that the crackdown by the Pakistani army in 1971 was justified to the West Pakistani public as a sort of *jihad*, or religious war. There is a further disturbing factor to this phenomenon, and that is its focus. Though one distinguishes between the three brands of Islam that are being propagated — political Islam, orthodox fundamentalist Islam and the syncretic fundamentalist Islam of the *pirs* — all have one common focus: women. Admittedly the first is placatory and attempts to reassure the women's movement that it is not 'against women' for all that it may be forging weapons that can be used by those who are. It is interesting that the focus is the same, although the constituencies of these three groups are not the same. The *pirs* control the credulous, be they educated or uneducated, though their largest following is among the un-educated; the orthodox fundamentalists control the educated lower middle class that feels alienated from political power; the military government essentially is protecting the special class interests. Thus those women who would oppose this triumvirate have to fight the battle on three fronts.

The women's movement

THE mainstream women's groups view these developments with mixed feel-ings. Despite following orthodox religious conventions such as fasting in Ramadan and being punctilious about prayers, rural women still follow many of the syncretic practices criticized by the early reformers.[12] As these practices are often degrading and some put the woman's life at risk, criticism of these customs as un-Islamic would serve some purpose. However, women's move-ment activists would rather use health as an argument. In any event, these contradictions do not trouble the self-appointed custodians of the faith. The sermons preached at their religious assemblies, which always concentrate on women and their behaviour, hardly ever condemn the practice of giving dowries at the time of marriage, which is definitely un-Islamic and has also been made illegal.[13] However, women practising birth control in the villages are routinely told that, if they continue, they will be denied burial according to Muslim rites.

Though of recent origin, the custom of dowry has taken firm root and flourishes apace. The Dowry Prohibition Act was passed in 1981. Offences under this Act were originally non-recognizable and hardly any action was taken under it. Even after the offence was made cognizable few cases were filed. As in India, the incidence of dowry appears to be increasing, as do crimes of violence against women by their husbands for failure of their parents to deliver the promised dowry. Legislation was passed on this account, too, and is known as The Cruelty to Women (Deterrent Punishment) Ordinance 1983. This is a tacit acknowledgement of the increase in crimes of violence against women but has not reduced the numbers of such acts. The ordinance also recognized dowry deaths as a specific category of criminal offence.

It may be argued that the Family Courts Ordinance of 1985, apparently passed in response to demands from the women's movement, is legislation that confers some benefit on women. In fact, it is a piece of window-dressing passed suddenly, shortly before a referendum in which the former President, Hussein Ershad, ostensibly received the people's mandate to hold elections under his aegis. No family courts were established. The ordinance merely designated the lowest subordinate civil court to hear only family matters on one specific day of the week. It should be noted that Bangladesh ratified, with reservations, the UN Convention for the Elimination of All Forms of Discrimination against Women where ratification would have meant taking steps to deal with the inequalities imposed upon women by the retention of personal laws derived from religious sources.

In urban areas, where these practices may not be so commonplace, there are other manifestations of un-Islamic behaviour for the righteous to seize upon. An example is dress; in particular, the *sari*. This was already labelled as un-Islamic attire in Zia-ul-Haq's Pakistan where women government servants were actually forbidden to wear *saris* to work. It was and is regarded as immodest in the Middle East. Now a subtle campaign was begun in Bangladesh to encourage women wearing *saris* to envelop themselves in shawl-like draperies reminis-cent of the Iranian *chador*. The women's pages of the fundamentalist papers and magazines harp on the theme of modesty in attire and submission of the wife to the husband. Thus the real cause of oppression of women is that they will argue with and contradict their husbands; if they kept quiet they would not be ill-treated. Purdah, they say, is not an impediment to women's emancipation, but rather it serves as protection for them. Men are not to be blamed for assaulting women when even saints have been tempted by abandonment in women. Therefore, women who are not properly covered, are, in the standard argument, asking for it.

During the 1990 parliamentary elections the two major political leaders were women. While it was not openly part of the various fundamentalists' political platform that a woman could not be head of state, both were criticized for moving 'freely' among men. That the parties led by these two women each attracted over 31 per cent of the votes cast and the religious party polled only 12 per cent would be reassuring if it were not for the fact that many of the first-time women voters were brought out to vote for the party 'that brought Islam back to Bangladesh'.[14] The women's movement, therefore, would appear to be up against a hydra-headed obscurantism.

What lies ahead?

IT IS difficult to predict how matters will develop in as volatile a place as Bangladesh. When Islam was made the state religion — by an amendment passed to the constitution — there was a lot of criticism from many quarters on the grounds that it was redundant, as 87 per cent of the population are Muslim, and hurtful to the sentiments of the 13 per cent who are not and who had fought in the war of liberation. There was a demonstration by a radical feminist group that has also filed a writ against the amendment. (This writ has not yet been heard.) But the largest women's organization, arguing that *prima facie* this would not be understood by the rank and file of its membership, was more reticent in its criticisms though it was, and continues to be, very active in mounting movements and demonstrations against *pirs* and others of that ilk who are guilty of misbehaviour such as rape. The example of the voting pattern of first-time women voters would appear to justify their caution. But, it points to a weakness in the movement that it allows the debate to go by default. The radical women would prefer to remove religion totally from the domain of politics. But this can be done only if it is made clear that being secular does not mean being irreligious. The distaste for what is seen as placating fanaticism or bigotry leaves the debate to the fundamentalist who never fails to stress that the slogan 'freedom of religion' is anti-Islam.

Where the women's movement exercises such caution, a political party, especially where it has canvassed for the women's vote on a note of religiosity, is unlikely to make any moves that could be misconstrued or give a handle to the fundamentalists. The devastating cyclone that hit Bangladesh just two months after the elections, provided grist to the fundamentalist mills of propaganda by way of a word-of-mouth whispering campaign which, in effect, sought to undermine morale by saying that this calamity was an Act of God's wrath for having a woman, and a widow, at the helm of affairs. None the less, the fact that the head of the party, who is the Prime Minister, is a woman will mean that such a government is less likely to take steps to curb women's political freedom. Of course, Britain's experience under a woman prime minister has shown that the sex of the premier executive is not, in itself, a factor in the liberation of women. Another comparison would be with Pakistan where Benazir Bhutto was able to do nothing for women, except to pass an amnesty releasing women who had been jailed under the Hudood Ordinances. Benazir, however, did not have an absolute majority in the assembly, Khaleda Zia does, but neither of the two main political parties in Bangladesh made women's rights a part of their manifesto.

The labour market could be a factor in emancipating women, inasmuch as the years of economic mismanagement have made it imperative for women to go out to work. But the fundamentalists have restructured their rhetoric to meet this challenge. While they still say that, in an ideal situation, women would stay at home fulfilling their divinely ordained role of mother and wife, they have had to admit tacitly that this is a difficult role to play if one has no male support. They have begun to say that there is no bar to women going out to work if circumstances necessitate this but that they should not work in an environment where there is no separation of sexes. There should be single-sex institutions — banks, hospitals, universities, and so on — for them; segregation should always be maintained. Given the exploitative conditions under which the bulk of women workers have to labour, it would not be surprising if the slogan to stay at home begins to have some appeal.

The ability of the fundamentalists to tailor their arguments to specific situations was demonstrated during the popular uprising that, in 1990, unseated the Ershad regime. One fundamentalist spokesman said that, while a Muslim woman could not aspire to the *imamate*, a woman head of state was preferable to an autocratic one. The issue of women being kept in their place was soft-pedalled during the uprising against the quasi-military undemocratic regime of President Ershad because it was being spearheaded by political parties led by women. But during the Ershad regime the fundamentalists had made the point that the 'reining in' of women was a necessary corollary to making Islam the state religion. A noteworthy comment in one of the fundamentalist papers on Women's International Day (8 March) was that no amount of rallies would safeguard the rights of women; only Islam could do so.

Conclusion

THE women's movement in Bangladesh — apart from the radical element which does not have a great following — has only taken on the fundamentalists on what might be called a personal level, which is easy enough since few of the leaders are personally admirable. These leaders are more frequently challenged for their deeds than for their words. But though this pragmatic approach is sensible given the ambiguity in most people about the degree to which they feel able to challenge the doctrines propounded by the fundamentalists, it is not enough. Until the doctrines themselves can be exposed for the illiterate cant that they are, the fundamentalist hold will not be weakened. The argument of radical women's groups, that countering the fundamentalist brand of religion with religious argument still leaves the door open to fundamentalism, is a cogent one. In the context of Bangladesh the question is whether there is any other choice.

Notes

1. The use of the term 'religious fundamentalism' in this chapter should not be taken to imply endorsement of the claim that the views of the fundamentalists reflect the essence or fundamentals of the religion. Most fundamentalists preach obscurantist doctrines.

2. David Abecassis, *Identity, Islam and Human Development in Rural Bangladesh* (Dhaka: University Press Ltd, 1990).

3. Lutful Kabir, *The Rights and Liabilities of the Raiyats Under the Bengal Tenancy Act 1885 and the State Acquisition and Tenancy Act 1950* (Dhaka: Law House Publication, 1972).

4. Manmohan Kaur, *Women in India's Freedom Struggle* (New Delhi: Sterling Publishers Ltd, 1985).

5. Maleka Begum, *Banglar Nari Andolar* (Dhaka: University Press Limited, 1990).

6. Purdah means, literally, curtain. Being in purdah refers to the custom of women living in seclusion. When such women travelled they would wear tent-like outer garments.

7. See Khawar Mumtaz and Farida Shaheed, *Women of Pakistan: Two Steps Forward, One Step Back?* (London: Zed Books, 1987).

8. The idea of an independent united Bengal was acceptable to the Muslim League (the political party that espoused the cause of the Muslims of India) because its leaders felt such an entity would veer towards Pakistan. By the same token, the idea of a united but independent Bengal was unacceptable to the Indian National Congress Party. In the

event, the latter view prevailed and Bengal was partitioned. See Harun-Or-Rashid, *The Foreshadowing of Bangladesh* (Dhaka: The Asiatic Society, 1987).

9. As early as February 1948 members of the Constituent Assembly were at loggerheads over the distribution of power between the two wings. Though the Muslim League itself had been formed in Bengal in 1926 by Nawab Salimuallah, the Nawab of Dhaka, the All-India leadership of the party was in the hands of politicians whose political base was not Bengal. There were Bengali politicians of sufficient stature to have challenged this leadership to the extent of getting a fair deal for Bengal but, in 1948, circumstances had temporarily neutralized them. The bureaucracy, which very quickly became the wielder of real power until displaced by the army, was drawn predominantly from the Punjab and from the United Provinces of India. (These provinces remained part of India but there were large-scale immigrations of Muslims from these to the west wing.)

10. By then democracy had been long dead, with the army in power since 1958 when it had toppled the government of a powerful East Pakistani prime minister. East and West Pakistan came together briefly in 1969 to challenge the president of the country, a general. He handed over power to his commander-in-chief, who promised elections. These were held at the end of 1970. The Awami League, an East Pakistan-based party, won all but two seats in the east wing giving them not only a majority in the province but the overall majority at the centre. This was unacceptable both to the army and to the majority party in the west wing, though not to the other West Pakistani political parties.

11. In the name of Allah the most merciful and most compassionate — a Muslim prayer.

12. Therese Blanchet, *Meanings and Rituals of Birth in Rural Bangladesh* (Dhaka: University Press Ltd, 1984).

13. Dowry-giving was not part of Muslim marriage in Bengal, indeed, it is not a Muslim practice. The groom, at the time of marriage, has to settle a sum of money on his bride — the *mahr*. This was the original pre-Islam brideprice, which was converted into a marriage settlement for the bride. The practice of the bride bringing a dowry is, of course, common in many societies. And as is evidenced in Jane Austen's novels, society more or less freely acknowledged that eligible young men looked for materially well-endowed brides, and it was difficult for girls without a 'portion' to find a spouse.

14. Report on Election to 5th Parliament 1991 BMNA (Bangladesh Mokti Nirbachan Andalon).

Chapter 5

Reform, revolution, and reaction: the trajectory of the 'Woman Question' in Afghanistan

Valentine M Moghadam

THIS chapter provides an historical perspective on the 'Woman Question' in Afghanistan, and seeks to explain why women's rights and women's emancipation have been such vexed issues. I hope to show that, notwithstanding the neglect of the gender dimension in nearly all accounts of Afghanistan, the woman question was an integral part of the conflict between the *mujahidin* and the ruling party, the People's Democratic Party of Afghanistan (PDPA), which came to power in the Saur (April) Revolution of 1978. The attempts by the PDPA to improve and enhance the status of women followed a Third World pattern of linking modernization, development, and socialism with women's emancipation, as was discussed in Chapter 1. Civil war in Afghanistan was to a great extent a battle between modern revolutionaries and traditional social groups. At the centre of the battle was the question of women.

I will argue here that the issue of women's rights in Afghanistan has been historically constrained by: a) the patriarchal nature of gender and social relations, deeply embedded in traditional communities, and b) the existence of a weak central state, which has been unable, since at least the beginning of this century, to implement modernizing programmes and goals in the face of 'tribal feudalism'. The two are interconnected, for the state's weakness is correlated with a strong (if fragmented) society resistant to state bureaucratic expansion, civil authority, regulation, monopoly of the means of violence, and extraction — the business of modern states. War, the fundamentalist backlash, and a hostile international setting eventually defeated the original goal of the emancipation of Afghan women. In the late 1980s, the Afghan leadership shifted from social revolution to national reconciliation, relegating the emancipation of women to a more stable future. And, in April 1992, the Government of Afghanistan collapsed and the *mujahidin* assumed control.

Afghanistan provides a vivid illustration of the stakes involved in contemporary debates on universalism versus cultural relativism, women's rights and community rights, the critique of orientalism and neo-colonialist discourses, the nature of Islamist movements, and reassessment of development. The section below will address some of these issues:

Eurocentrism or universalist values

The novel character of the new regime [in Afghanistan] soon became apparent. It committed itself to land reform, to equality of the nationalities, to emancipating women, to a solution of the nomadic question. So it was that, at a time and in a place suspected by few, and in a country renowned only for colonial war and narcotic plenitude, a revolutionary process of some description had begun.

Fred Halliday, 'Revolution in Afghanistan', *New Left Review* 112 (November/December 1978), p. 3.

... such proposed reforms, casting the issues of poverty and women's status into a basically First World perspective, may be seen as a radical improvement from the legislators' point of view, but this perspective has many critics in the Third World and elsewhere.

Nancy Tapper, 'Causes and Consequences of the Abolition of Brideprice in Afghanistan', in M Nazif Shahrani and Robert Canfield (eds.) *Revolutions and Rebellions in Afghanistan* , (Berkeley: Institute of International Studies, University of California, 1984), p. 291.

The *mujahideen* recognize women's importance to the *jihad* (holy war) with their exhortations to preserve women's honor through the continued practice of seclusion. The reinforcement of this tradition, most Westerners have failed to notice, serves to strengthen the men's will to resist ... Purdah provides the opportunity for preserving one's own identity and a certain stability in the face of external pressures ... Westerners who have been quick to impose their own ethnocentric perceptions should note the value of this seemingly anachronistic custom for a people under siege whose very survival is at stake.

Kathleen Howard-Merriam, 'Afghan Women and Their Struggle for Survival', in Grant Farr and John Merriam (eds.) *The Afghan Conflict: The Politics of Survival* (Boulder, Colo: Westview Press, 1987), p. 114.

The customs of former times might be said to be too simple and barbaric. For Greeks used to go around armed with swords; and they used to buy wives from one another; and there are surely other ancient customs that are extremely stupid (for example, in Cyme there is a law about homicide, that if a man prosecuting a charge can produce a certain number of witnesses from among his own relations, the defendant will automatically be convicted of murder). In general, all human beings seek not only the way of their ancestors, but the good.

Aristotle, *Politics*, cited in Martha Nussbaum, 'Non-Relative Virtues: An Aristotelian Approach' (WIDER Working Paper no. 32, Dec. 1987), p. 5.

You report the proclamation of a 'free Muslim state' by the Afghan guerrilla leaders seeking international recognition of their 'government-in-exile' [February 1989]. Free for whom, free for what? ... Afghan women are conspicuously without a voice in the formation of a 'cabinet'. A theology professor has been named 'acting prime minister'. He is backed by Saudi Arabia, and you describe him as a 'strict fundamentalist who opposes educating women and refuses to give interviews to journalists who are women'. Nor were women heard in the choice of the fundamentalist who would head the justice ministry. Justice for whom? Women in the United States who knew the rebels' resistance toward women's rights winced at the euphemism 'freedom fighters'. They must now feel doubly affronted on behalf of their Afghan sisters, who will be forced to live in a 'free Muslim state' which interprets the Koran's teachings in a way that abjures gender parity even at elementary levels of education and occupation, let alone government leadership.

Rose M Somerville, Letter to the Editor, *New York Times*, 18 April 1989.

Can the evolution of the condition of women in the Arab world be evaluated by the same criteria as in the West? Is it not Eurocentric to put forward the lives of Western women as the only democratic, just, and forward-looking model? I do not think so. The demands of Western feminists seem to me to represent the greatest advance toward the emancipation of people.

Juliette Minces, *The House of Obedience: Women in Arab Society* (London: Zed Books, 1982), p. 25.

The preceding quotations capture the complexity of the issues involved. Should progressives support liberation movements that deny women any voice, let alone rights? Is it Eurocentric to propose that the status of women in Afghanistan is low, and that it can and should be improved through universal education, rural development, and legal reform? Are those of us who propose such changes and reforms merely imposing our own urban middle-class or élite assumptions on rural peoples? Are there divergent First World and Third World perspectives on women's status? Is it not possible to criticize unequal and oppressive gender relations in Muslim societies without being labelled orientalist? Are there no universal values or criteria?

My own answers to these questions will be evident in the course of this chapter. Through an examination of the nature of Afghan patriarchy, and an historical survey of government efforts to modernize and develop the country, including reforms to raise the status of women, I shall try to place the 1978-79 reforms in historical and social perspective.

Social structure in Afghanistan

Tribal formations and the patriarchal household

HISTORICALLY, the population of Afghanistan has been fragmented into myriad ethnic, linguistic, religious, kin-based, and regional groupings.[1] 'Afghan nationalism' properly speaking is at best incipient, as the concept of a nation-state, or of a national identity, is absent for much of the population, and has been promoted primarily by modernizing élites since the nineteenth century.[2] During most of the country's recent history, the fragmented groupings composed warring factions. Battles were fought principally over land and water, sometimes women and 'honour', usually sheer power — or what Massell, writing of early twentieth-century Central Asia, described as primordial cleavages and conflicts.[3]

One of the few commonalities in this diverse country is Islam. Afghan Islam is a unique combination of practices and precepts from the *Sharia* (Islamic canon law as delineated in religious texts) and tribal customs, particularly Pushtunwali, the tribal code of the Pushtuns, who comprise about 50 per cent of the population. On certain issues, Pushtunwali and Islam disagree.[4] For example, the absence of inheritance rights for females is contrary to Islamic law but integral to the complex web of the tribal exchange system. Contrary to the

Islamic ban on usury, there has been widespread usury, and this practice has kept rural households in perpetual indebtedness. Exorbitant expenditure in marriages (for example, on dower such as *sheer-baha* and *walwar*) has also contributed to the rural household's debt accumulation. The Islamic dower, *mahr*, has been abused. *Mahr* is a payment due from groom to bride which is an essential part of the formal Islamic marriage contract. In the Quran it is a nominal fee and in many Muslim countries its purpose is to provide a kind of social insurance for the wife in the event of divorce or widowhood. In the Afghan patriarchal context, the *mahr* (or *walwar* in Pashtu) is the payment to the bride's father as compensation for the loss of his daughter's labour in the household unit.[5]

Afghan rural and poor women work extraordinarily hard, but their ability to contribute substantially to household survival or the family income takes place within a patriarchal context of women's subordination and intra-household inequality. In such a context, a woman's labour power is controlled and allocated by someone other than herself, the products of her labour are managed by others, and she receives no remuneration for work performed. In areas where carpet-making is a commercial enterprise, male kin are allowed to exploit women's labour without any wage payment, as Afshar has found for Iran and Berik has described for Turkey. In extended patriarchal, patrilineal households, as Kandiyoti has argued, collective (male) interests dictate strict control of female labour deployment throughout a woman's lifetime.[6]

Contemporary Afghanistan is situated in what the demographer John Caldwell has called 'the patriarchal belt', and is an extreme case of what Kandiyoti calls 'classic patriarchy'.[7] This belt stretches from northern Africa across the Middle East to the northern plains of the Indian subcontinent and parts of (rural) China. Here the patriarchal extended family is the central social unit, in which the senior man has authority over everyone else, including younger men, and women are subject to distinct forms of control and subordination. Young brides marry into large families, gain respect mainly via their sons, and late in life acquire power as mothers-in-law. The social structures in the patriarchal belt are characterized by their institutionalization of extremely restrictive codes of behaviour for women, such as the practice of rigid gender segregation and a powerful ideology linking family honour to female virtue. Men are entrusted with safeguarding family honour through their control over female members; they are backed by complex social arrangements which ensure the protection — and dependence — of women. In contemporary

Muslim patriarchal societies, such control over women is considered necessary in part because women are regarded as the potential source of social *fitna*, that is, disorder or anarchy.[8]

Women's life-chances are severely circumscribed by the patriarchal arrangements that favour men. One typically finds an adverse sex ratio, low female literacy and educational attainment, high fertility rates, high maternal mortality rates, and low female labour-force participation in the formal sector. Demographic facts about societies such as Afghanistan, Pakistan, and north India suggest 'a culture against women', in which women are socialized to sacrifice their health, survival chances, and life options.[9]

Afghan patriarchy is tied to the prevalence of such forms of subsistence as nomadic pastoralism, herding and farming, and settled agriculture, all organized along patrilineal lines. Historically, Afghan gender roles and women's status have been tied to property relations. Property includes live-stock, land, and houses or tents. Women and children tend to be assimilated into the concept of property and to belong to a male. This is particularly the case among Pashtuns, whose tribal culture, Pushtunwali, is highly masculinist. Tapper writes of the Durrani Pashtuns of north-central Afghanistan: 'The members of the community discuss control of all resources — especially labour, land, and women — in terms of honor.'[10] Note that 'community' is the community of men, and that 'women' are assimilated in the concept of 'resources'. Griffiths describes a conversation with the governor of a district in Kunduz, who explained with some pride

> how five or six women might work together for four or five months to make a patterned carpet ... and how a man would pay a very good brideprice for a girl who was an accomplished carpet weaver. When I asked him who got the money for the carpets, he looked at me in astonishment and replied: 'Why the man of course, the woman belongs to the man.' This is the attitude which is the chief obstacle facing the champions of women's emancipation in Afghanistan.[11]

Gender segregation and female seclusion exist, though they vary by ethnic group, region, mode of subsistence, social class, and family. Boesen has noted a Pashtun saying that 'a woman is best either in the house or in the grave'. Others have emphasized the system of purdah, referring to both the all-enveloping *burqa*, a tent-like garment worn over the head with only a small grille-type opening for the eyes, and the seclusion and isolation of women. This seclusion from the world outside the family walls is customarily justified by invoking Quranic prescription and by the notion that women are basically licentious and tempt men. Purdah is characteristic of townspeople and settled agriculturalists rather than the Durrani nomads described by Tapper. Even so, Tapper writes of a rigid sexual division of labour that confines women to the domestic sphere:

> Men do all the work of agriculture and house construction, and tend, shear and butcher animals; they market produce and buy all foodstuffs and other supplies. Women rear young children, cook and clean, process milk, spin and weave ... Women's involvement in co-operation outside the household is by contrast very limited. They may act as domestic servants for women in other households, but most often only as an incidental consequence of an economic contract between the husbands. In short the women's productive activities all take place within the domestic sphere and the fruits of their labour are destined almost entirely for domestic consumption or use.[12]

According to one account, women are regarded as *naqis-e-aql* [stupid by birth], and the term 'woman' is often used by men intending to insult opponents. In a pattern typical of South Asia (notably India) rather than of Muslim countries in general, families celebrate the birth of a boy but not that of a girl. Again, similar to India, marriages are arranged, often at childhood. Strict social traditions confine women to their homes and forbid them to talk to men — except for immediate relatives. If a woman talks to a stranger or is suspected of complicity in a sexual affair, she is condemned to death. According to Emadi, a woman has no right to protest or to defend herself against injustices, or to seek divorce. It is a disgrace for a woman to protest physical and mental abuse by her father, brother or husband.[13]

Veronica Doubleday, who lived in Herat on and off between 1972 and 1977, explains in her book that women's complaints focused around two issues, which she came to see as related: sickness and the restrictions imposed by their seclusion. The women complained of backaches, lack of energy and many other ailments, and said that sometimes their husbands would not let them go to a doctor. Some women complained specifically about their seclusion, which they called *qeit*, or confinement, imprisonment. Doubleday describes how, despite her desire to avoid Western ethnocentrism, she had to conclude that purdah was not simply about being segregated and veiled; it meant that men had complete control over the movements of their women, giving them ultimate power. She also describes 'the deep anxiety women experienced over illness'. She writes:

> As mothers and nurturers of the family they had a vital responsibility, and yet they and their children were especially vulnerable since they depended upon their husbands for money for cures. It was iniquitous but true that men could deny women and children recourse to medical help, and it was no wonder that women placed importance upon methods such as divination or diet, which were at least accessible and within their control.[14]

Economic dependence on men, the practice of seclusion, and high maternal mortality may explain why census and surveys undertaken in 1967, 1972-74 and 1979 revealed an unusually high ratio of males to females, which even exceeded the expected under-reporting of females in a conservative Islamic society.[15]

And what of women's resistance, and their own aspirations? Boesen reports that women resent male control of their sexuality and they rebel, pursuing extramarital affairs and covering up each other's activities. Such forms of resistance, however, do not challenge gender status ranking. Although Tapper has stated that a typical Afghan woman's wish is for a successful marriage with many sons, Doubleday's book on women in Herat reveals that women also have other aspirations, but that these are blocked.[16]

A final word on marriage and brideprice is necessary, in order to put in perspective the reformers' measures against them. In a patriarchal context, marriage and brideprice are a transaction between households, an integral part of property relations and the exchange system, and an indicator of status. In Afghanistan, marriage, forced or voluntary, is a way of ending feuds, cementing a political alliance between families, increasing the family's prestige, or accumulating wealth. Mobility and migration patterns also revolve around the brideprice; men from one region will travel to another to find inexpensive brides, while other men will travel elsewhere because they can obtain a higher price for their daughters. The heaviest expenses any household has to bear are concerned with marriage. The choice of bride, the agreed brideprice, and the time taken to complete a marriage may visibly confirm or, indeed, increase a household's poverty. Tapper's description accords well with the discussion by Massell of the importance of *Kalym* (brideprice) to overall property relations in early twentieth-century Central Asia.[17] But it also reveals the extent to which the exchange of women for brideprice, or in compensation for blood, treats women exclusively as reproducers and pawns in economic and political exchanges.

Strong society, weak state

AFGHANISTAN is a prototypical 'weak state', inasmuch as the central authorities have been unable to realize their goals, or to regulate social relations and use resources in determined ways.[18] The existence of a weak modern state in a predominantly patriarchal and tribal society has had adverse implications for reform and development, as well as for the advancement of women. Since modernization began in the mid-nineteenth century, various governments and rulers have sought to discourage excessive expenditure on brideprice and marriage celebrations as a way of preventing rural indebtedness; and they have tried to extend education to girls. Various state initiatives this century have invariably resulted in tribal rebellion to government authority.[19] Although Afghanistan was not immune to the general process of social change enveloping Muslim countries, it has seen less transformation than neighbouring countries. Gregorian explains:

> For most of the nineteenth century, Afghanistan remained culturally one of the most isolated and parochial regions of the Muslim world, almost totally cut off from the mainstream of European thought. It did not undergo any direct and intensive experience of European colonial rule; on the contrary, imperialism, while impressing on Afghans the necessity of technological borrowing, contributed to Afghan political and cultural isolationism.[20]

British attempts to expand their sphere of influence outward from India led to two Anglo-Afghan wars (1839 and 1879), which contributed to the growth of a politico-religious nationalism and xenophobia. Moreover, the struggle strengthened the position of the Afghan tribes and the monarchy's dependence on their military might, and reinforced the position of the Afghan religious establishment. Gregorian states that in the absence of noteworthy learning institutions, a secular intelligentsia, or reformist movements among the Afghan *ulama*, the formulation and propagation of the aims of Afghan nationalism and modernism came late. The two causes were not linked until the first two decades of the twentieth century, when a small group of educated

Afghans sought to broaden the base of support for political and economic reform by merging the two movements. Under the leadership of the King, Amanullah (1919-29), these Young Afghans, like the Young Turks near by, made ambitious plans for the modernization of the country, explicitly including the emancipation of women in their agenda, as was the case in Ataturk's Turkey. Their ultimate failure, Gregorian notes, determined the course and nature of all future reforms and modernization programmes in Afghanistan. According to Urban, the record of Afghanistan's leaders until 1978 was a pitiful one: they had failed to give the country any of the attributes of the modern centralized state.[21]

One example of state failure was in education. The first secondary school (for boys only) was established in 1904 and was called Habibiyeh College after its patron, Habibullah Khan. In 1913 the Afghan Department of Education was founded. In 1922, Amanullah Khan established the Amaniyeh School, later renamed Lycée Esteqlal, and founded Essmat (later renamed Malalai) School for girls, which was closed after his downfall/abdication. The foundations of Kabul University were laid in 1932, when what was to become its first faculty, the School of Medicine, was established. Malalai School was reopened in the 1930s under Nadir Shah but, according to Gregorian, it was promoted as a special school for nurses and midwives in order to soften the opposition of the *mullahs* (clerics) and the other traditionalists. It was to be some two decades before Malalai would become a true secondary school and produce its first graduates.[22] As late as 1954, the total student enrolment in Afghanistan, excluding the students at Kabul University, was 114,266, or about 4.5 per cent of the approximately 2.4 million school-age children.[23] At that time there were only 13 primary schools, one middle school, and two secondary schools for girls, most of them in Kabul, and only an estimated 8,625 girls were receiving any kind of education. There were reportedly no girls in the village schools.[24]

Early reforms and tribal reaction

REFORMS to improve the status of women began during the reign of Abdur Rahman Khan, who ascended the throne in 1880. He abolished a long-standing customary law which, in violation of Islamic law, bound a wife not only to her husband but to his entire family as well: widows who wanted to remarry had to marry their husbands' next of kin, often against their will.[25] Abdur Rahman decreed that the moment a husband died his wife was to be set free, although there was no way to check to what extent this law was enforced. Among Abdur

Rahman's other measures was a law requiring the registration of marriages (*sabt*). He also modified a law pertaining to child marriages, permitting a girl, who had been given in marriage before she had reached the age of puberty, to refuse or accept her marriage ties when she attained full age. Still another law allowed women to sue their husbands for alimony or divorce in cases involving cruelty or non-support.[26]

Mahmud Tarzi (1866-1935), royal adviser and editor of *Siraj al-Akhbar Afghaniyah*, a bi-weekly paper and forum for the Young Afghans, appealed for compulsory education, including that of girls. According to Gregorian, he was the first Afghan to take a positive stand on feminism, dedicating a series of articles to famous women in history that discussed the many abilities of women. A monogamist himself, Tarzi never explicitly attacked polygamy, but he did so implicitly by constantly referring to the idéal family as one in which there was one wife and a few children. Since in his view the health, welfare and education of Afghan families was essential to Afghan progress, he attacked the expenditure incurred in connection with multiple marriages, which often ruined families financially.[17]

In 1922, Habibullah Khan attempted to limit the expenses incurred in connection with marriage, which led most Afghans to borrow money, at times paying as much as 75 per cent interest on the loan. Habibullah placed a ceiling on the amount that could be spent, urging his people to abandon the customary public celebrations in favour of private parties. The amounts he set varied according to class. Gregorian doubts that the law was strictly enforced, but notes that on a few highly publicized occasions the royal family attempted to set an example for the rest of Afghan society. The Amir also tried to set an example to the wealthy Afghans who exceeded the legal limit of four wives. Officially banning the practice of keeping concubines and 'female slaves', Habibullah publicly divorced all but four of his wives in 1903.[28]

By establishing Habibiyeh College, Habibullah also sought to broaden the education system. Despite the founding of the Afghan Department of Education, government attempts to improve and standardize the curriculum were not totally successful. Gregorian writes that the *mullahs*, especially those outside Kabul, resented the government's control of education, the teacher-training centre, and the teaching of English and of modern subjects in general, and vehemently resisted all further innovation.[29]

Habibullah Khan was assassinated in 1919. His son, King Amanullah, had the enormous task of convincing the religious establishment that modern secular education and Islam were not incompatible, and that the schools he built did not threaten the sanctity or spiritual message of Islam.[30] His most audacious act was to begin a study-abroad programme for Afghan students, and to open the first schools for girls. By 1928 there were about 800 girls attending schools in Kabul and there were even some Afghan women studying abroad, notably in Turkey, France, and Switzerland. Gregorian notes that Amanullah had plans to build five more schools for girls and intended his planned compulsory education system to apply to girls as well as boys. But both efforts were dropped after his fall in 1929.

In examining Amanullah's reform programme and organized resistance to it, one discovers parallels with the experience of the PDPA government some 50 years later. According to Gregorian, Amanullah's general programme to improve the position of women was promoted by his wife, Queen Soraya (who founded the first women's magazine, *Ershad-e Niswan*), the reformer Mahmud Tarzi and his wife, the small intelligentsia, and the modernist and nationalist Young Afghans, impressed by developments in Turkey, Iran and Egypt. In 1921, Amanullah enacted the Family Code, which undertook to regulate marriages and engagements. Child marriages and intermarriage between close kin were outlawed as contrary to Islamic principles. In the new code Amanullah reiterated Abdur Rahman's ruling that a widow was to be free of the domination of her husband's family. He followed his father's example and placed tight restrictions on wedding expenses, including dowries, and granted wives the right to appeal to the courts if their husbands did not adhere to Quranic tenets regarding marriage. In the autumn of 1924, Afghan girls were given the right to choose their husbands, a measure that incensed the traditionalists.[31]

The presence in Kabul of a considerable number of unveiled women, especially Turkish women who had abandoned the veil and adopted modern dress, undoubtedly encouraged the efforts of the new Afghan feminists. However, their greatest support came from Amanullah, who believed the key to the future structure of Afghanistan would be the emancipation of women.[32]

The Afghan press, including bulletins of the War Office, took part in the emancipation campaign. In 1928, during the·final months of his rule, King Amanullah made a frontal assault against the institution of purdah, which 'hid half the Afghan nation'. Because of his efforts and the example of Queen Soraya, some 100 Afghan women had reportedly discarded the veil by October 1928.

By this time, Afghan legislation was among the most progressive in the

Muslim world. No other country had addressed the sensitive issues of child marriage and polygamy. Afghan family law on these issues became the model for similar reforms in Soviet Central Asia in 1926.[33] It is not surprising that the family law of 1921 was a major cause of the uprising instigated by the clergy in 1924.

The first organized reaction against the Amanullah reforms was directed against a controversial administrative code, the *Nizam-nameh*, which he passed in 1923. Among other things, the code attempted to liberalize the position of women and to permit the government to regulate the various family problems formerly dealt with by the local *mullah*. A few traditionalist *mullahs* inveighed against the new code, asserting that it was contrary to the precepts of Islamic law. Their cause was picked up in 1924 by the Mangal tribe of the Khost region and soon assumed dangerous proportions. By March armed warfare had broken out. The religious and tribal leaders of the revolt were particularly exercised over the sections of the code that deprived men of full authority over their wives and daughters, an authority that had been sanctioned by time-honoured custom. They were further incensed at the opening of public schools for girls.

The Khost rebellion continued for more than nine months and illustrated dramatically the weakness of the Afghan army. Gregorian writes that King Amanullah was forced to fall back on levies from certain tribes and proclaim a *jihad* before he was able to suppress the revolt. The rebels suffered enormous losses, as did the government side. The cost of the rebellion represented the total government receipts for two years. As a result the King was forced to postpone various modernization projects and revoke or modify many important sections of the *Nizam-nameh*; the schooling of girls, for example, was limited to the under-12 age group. In 1928 the *Loya Jirga*, the traditional Afghan consultative body, rejected Amanullah's proposal to set an age limit on marriage, which the King suggested should be 18 for girls and 20 for men. They also vehemently opposed the notion of a modern, Western education for Afghan girls, either in Afghanistan or outside it.

In the autumn of 1928, a group of female students was sent to Turkey for higher education, and the Association for the Protection of Women's Rights (*Anjoman-i Hemayat-i Neswan*) was established to help women fight domestic injustice and take a role in public life. The Queen presided over several committees to strengthen the emancipation campaign. These unprecedented measures, which violated traditional norms, offended the religious leaders and their following, especially in rural areas. Reaction against the campaign for women's emancipation was a major factor in the outbreak of the violent disturbances in November and December of 1928.

When the King banned the practice of polygamy among government officials it caused an uproar among the religious establishment. A tribal revolt ensued, led by Bacha-i Saqqo, a Tajik rebel claiming Islamic credentials. As the political situation deteriorated, Amanullah was compelled to cancel most of his social reforms and to suspend his controversial administrative measures. The Afghan girls studying in Constantinople were to be recalled, and the schools for girls were to be closed; women were not to go unveiled or cut their hair; the *mullahs* were no longer to be required to obtain teaching certificates, while compulsory military recruitment was to be abandoned and the old tribal system reinstated.[34]

As a last, desperate, concession, the unhappy Amir agreed to the formation of a council of 50 notables, to be chosen from among 'the most respected religious luminaries and tribal chieftains', and promised to abide by their advice as well as to conform to Islamic law as interpreted by the orthodox religious leaders. Any measure the government proposed to enact was to be ratified by this council. But in the end, all of these concessions were to no avail. The rebels attacked Kabul, Amanullah abdicated and left Afghanistan.

Not until the 1950s were reforms attempted again. In 1950 a law was passed banning ostentatious lifecycle ceremonies. It prohibited many of the expensive aspects of birth, circumcision, marriage and burial rituals, but was difficult to enforce. The Marriage Law of 1971 once again tried to curb the indebtedness arising from the costs of marriage. The Civil Law of 1977 abolished child marriage and established 16 as the minimum age of marriage for girls. But the law remained weak and was ignored. Furthermore, the law left the husband's right to unilateral divorce basically untouched.[35]

The historical background presented above suggests the enormous difficulty faced by Afghan modernizers. The Afghan state had been too weak to implement reforms or to undertake modernization in an effective way, and was constantly confronted by religious-tribal forces seeking to prevent any change whatsoever, particularly in their power.

Nevertheless, as in many other Third World countries during the 1960s, a left-wing modernizing élite organized itself to address the country's problems and to steer Afghanistan away from its dependency on aid from the United States.

The Saur Revolution and women's rights

IN 1965, a group from the small Afghan intelligentsia formed the People's Democratic Party of Afghanistan (PDPA). Evoking the Amanullah experiment, the PDPA envisaged a national democratic government to liberate Afghanistan from backwardness. Among its demands were primary education for all children in their mother tongue and the development of the different languages and cultures of the country. Its social demands included guarantees of the right to work, equal treatment for women, a 42-hour working week, paid sickness and maternity leave, and a ban on child labour. That same year, six women activists formed the Democratic Organization of Afghan Women (DOAW). The DOAW's main objectives were to eliminate illiteracy among women, forced marriages, and the brideprice. As a result of the activities of the DOAW and the PDPA, and notwithstanding hostility from *mullahs* and other conservatives, women won the right to vote and, in the 1970s, four women from the DOAW were elected to parliament. In the years before the Saur Revolution, the DOAW managed to win the legal right of women to study abroad and to seek employment outside the home, previously the privilege of a few women from élite families. Both the PDPA and the DOAW were eager for more profound, extensive, and permanent changes.[36]

Among the most remarkable and influential of the DOAW activists was Anahita Ratebzad. In the 1950s she studied nursing in the United States, and then returned to Kabul as director and instructor of nursing at the Women's Hospital. Nancy Dupree notes that when the faculty for women at Kabul University was established, she entered the medical college and became a member of its teaching staff after graduating in 1963. She joined the PDPA in 1965, and was one of the four female candidates for parliament. This was the first time liberals and leftists had openly appeared in the political arena. They encountered strong reaction on the part of conservative members of parliament. In 1968 the latter proposed to enact a law prohibiting Afghan girls from studying abroad. Hundreds of girls demonstrated in opposition. In 1970 two reactionary *mullahs* protested such public evidence of female liberation as miniskirts, women teachers, and schoolgirls by shooting at the legs of women in Western dress and splashing them with acid. Among those who joined in this action was Gulbeddin Hekmatyar (who went on to be a leading figure in the *mujahidin*, one of the 'freedom fighters' hailed by President Reagan). This time there was a protest demonstration of 5,000 girls.[37]

In April 1978, the PDPA seized power in what came to be called the Saur (April) Revolution, and introduced a reform programme to change the political and social structure of Afghan society. Three decrees — Nos. 6, 7, and 8 — were the main planks of the programme of social and economic reform. Decree No. 6 was intended to put an end to land mortgage and indebtedness; No. 7 was designed to stop the payment of brideprice and give women more freedom of choice in marriage; No. 8 consisted of rules and regulations for the confiscation and redistribution of land.[38] The three decrees were complementary, but Decree No. 7 seems to have been the most controversial. In a speech on 4 November 1978, President Noor Mohammad Taraki declared: 'Through the issuance of Decrees No. 6 and 7, the hard-working peasants were freed from bonds of oppressors and money-lenders, ending the sale of girls for good as hereafter nobody would be entitled to sell any girl or woman in this country.'[39] The six articles of Decree No. 7 were as follows:

Article 1. No one shall engage a girl or give her in marriage in exchange for cash or commodities.
Article 2. No one shall compel the bridegroom or his guardians to give holiday presents to the girl or her family.
Article 3. The girl or her guardian shall not take cash or commodities in the name of dower (*mahr*) in excess of ten dirham [Arabic coinage] according to *Sharia* (Islamic law), which is not more than 300 afs. [about US $10] on the basis of the bank rate of silver.
Article 4. Engagements and marriage shall take place with the full consent of the parties involved: (a) No one shall force marriage; (b) No one shall prevent the free marriage of a widow or force her into marriage because of family relationships (the levirate) or patriarchal ties; (c) No one shall prevent legal marriages on the pretext of engagement, forced engagement expenses, or by using force.
Article 5. Engagement and marriages for women under 16 and men under 18 are not permissible.
Article 6. (1) Violators shall be liable to imprisonment from six months to three years; (2) Cash or commodities accepted in violation of the provisions of this decree shall be confiscated.[40]

The PDPA government also embarked on an aggressive campaign for literacy led by the DOAW, whose function was to educate women, bring them out of seclusion, and initiate social programmes. PDPA cadre established literacy classes for men, women, and children in villages, and by August 1979 the government had established 600 new schools.[41]

This was clearly an audacious programme for social change, one aimed at the rapid transformation of a patriarchal society and a decentralized power structure based on tribal and landlord authority. Revolutionary change, state-building, and women's rights subsequently went hand-in-hand. The emphasis on women's rights by the PDPA reflected: (a) their socialist/Marxist ideology; (b) their modernizing and egalitarian outlook; (c) their social base and origins — urban middle-class professionals, educated in the US, USSR, India, and Western and Eastern Europe; (d) the influence of its women members.

In 1976 Anahita Ratebzad had been elected to the central committee of the PDPA. After the Saur Revolution, she was elected to the Revolutionary Council of the Democratic Republic of Afghanistan (DRA) and appointed Minister of Social Affairs. Other influential PDPA women in the Taraki government (April 1978—September 1979) were Sultana Umayd, Director of Kabul Girls' School; Soraya, president of the DOAW; Ruhafza Kamyar, principal of the DOAW's Vocational High School; Firouza, director of the Afghan Red Crescent (Red Cross); Dilara Mahak, principal of the Amana Fidawa School; Professor Mrs R S Siddiqui (who was especially outspoken in her criticism of 'feudalistic patriarchal relations'). In the Amin government (September-December 1979), the following women headed schools and the women's organization, as well as sitting on government sub-committees: Fawjiyah Shahsawari, Dr Aziza, Shirin Afzal, Alamat Tolqun. These were the women who were behind the programme for women's rights. Their intention was to expand literacy, especially for girls and women, encourage income-generating projects and employment for women, provide health and legal services for women, and eliminate those aspects of Muslim family law which discriminate against women — unilateral male repudiation, father's exclusive rights to child custody, unequal inheritance, and male guardianship over women.

Patriarchal resistance to change

PDPA attempts to change marriage laws, expand literacy, and educate rural girls met with strong opposition. Decrees 6 and 7 deeply angered rural tribesmen and the traditional power structure. Fathers with unmarried daughters resented the decree most because they could no longer expect to receive brideprice payments for them when they did marry. In particular, Decree No. 7 was unpopular because it represented a threat to male honour.

According to Beattie: 'By banning brideprice — and especially by declaring women could marry whom they pleased — it threatened to undermine the strict control over women on which the maintenance of male honour depended.'[42] Believing that women should not appear at public gatherings, villagers often refused to attend classes after the first day. PDPA cadre viewed this attitude as retrograde and, thus, the cadre resorted to different forms of persuasion, including physical force, to make the villagers return to literacy classes. Often PDPA cadre were either kicked out of the village or murdered. In the summer of 1978 refugees began pouring into Pakistan, giving as the main reason forceful implementation of the literacy programme among their women. In Kandahar, three literacy workers from the women's organization were killed as symbols of the unwanted revolution. Two men killed all the women in their families to prevent them from 'dishonour'.[43] An Islamist opposition began organizing and conducted several armed actions against the government in spring 1979.

The right of women to divorce was one of the most significant measures introduced by the PDPA. Although the divorce law was never officially announced owing to the outbreak of tribal Islamist opposition to the regime, the family courts (*mahakem-i famili*), mostly presided over by female judges, provided hearing sessions for discontented wives and sought to protect their rights to divorce and on issues such as alimony, child custody, and child support.

Internal battles within the PDPA (especially between its two wings, Parcham and Khalq) exacerbated the government's difficulties. In September 1979, President Taraki was killed on the orders of his deputy, Hafizullah Amin, a ruthless and ambitious man who imprisoned and executed hundreds of his own comrades in addition to further alienating the population.[44] The Pakistani regime of Zia ul-Haq was opposed to leftists next door, and supported the *mujahidin* armed uprising. In December 1979 the Soviet army intervened, beginning a long military engagement in the country's civil war on the side of the PDPA government. Amin was killed and succeeded by Babrak Karmal, who initiated what was called 'the second phase' (*marhale-i dovvom*). The civil war continued, and was internationalized, with the *mujahidin* receiving support not only from Pakistan but also Saudi Arabia, the Islamic Republic of Iran, China, and the United States.

PDPA and DOAW attempts to extend literacy to rural girls have been widely criticized for heavy-handedness by most commentators on Afghanistan. Three points regarding this criticism are in order. First, literacy campaigns are common during or following popular revolutions and movements for national or social liberation: the Bolsheviks, Chinese, Cubans, Vietnamese, Angolans, Palestinians, Eritreans, and Nicaraguans had extensive literacy campaigns. Second, the PDPA's rationale for pursuing the rural literacy campaign with some zeal was that all previous reformers had made literacy a matter of choice; male guardians had chosen not to allow their females to be educated; thus 98 per cent of all Afghan women were illiterate. It was decided therefore not to allow literacy to remain a matter of (men's) choice, but rather a matter of principle and law. A third point is that state coercion to raise the status of women has been undertaken elsewhere, notably Soviet Central Asia and Turkey in the 1920s. And other governments have issued decrees that have been resisted — for example, in the United States, emancipation of slaves, state-ordered school segregation and forced busing in the 1960s and 1970s, and the periodic attacks on Mormon polygamous units. This is not to condone the use of force, but to point out that rights, reforms, and revolutions have been effected coercively or attained through struggle.

It should be noted that not everyone in the PDPA and the DOAW was in favour of the pace of the reforms. According to Soraya, many DOAW activists, including herself, were opposed to the pace and the compulsory nature of the programme for land reform, women's education, and the new family law. As a result of her antagonism toward Hafizullah Amin, Soraya, like many PDPA members of the Parcham wing, was imprisoned, and even endured torture. She, along with the others, was released after the Soviet intervention, the death of Amin, and his replacement by Babrak Karmal.[45]

In 1980, the PDPA slowed its reform programme and announced its intention to eliminate illiteracy in the cities in seven years and in the provinces in ten. In an interview that year Anahita Ratebzad conceded errors, 'in particular the compulsory education of women', to which she added, 'the reactionary elements immediately made use of these mistakes to spread discontent among the population'.[46] Despite the slowing of reforms (including concessions such as the restoration of Muslim family law),[47] the Peshawar-based opposition intensified their efforts to destroy the Kabul regime, supported by Pakistan, the United States, China, the Islamic Republic of Iran, and Saudi Arabia. In contrast to the Iranian state next door, the Afghan state was unable to impose its will through an extensive administrative and military apparatus. As a result, the programme on land redistribution and women's rights faltered. The efforts of the government to raise women's status through legal changes relating to marriage were stymied by patriarchal structures highly resistant to change, by a hostile international environment, and by an extremely destructive civil war.

The literature on Afghanistan has been exceedingly partisan, and much of it very pro-*mujahidin*, with a noticeable reluctance to discuss the positive aspects of the PDPA state's social programme, notably its policy on women's rights. One political journalist has written, however, that the 'one genuine achievement of the revolution has been the emancipation of (mainly urban) women'. He continued: 'There is no doubt that thousands of women are committed to the regime, as their prominent participation in Revolutionary Defence Group militias shows. Eyewitnesses stated that militant militiawomen played a key role in defending the besieged town of Urgun in 1983. Four of the seven militia commanders appointed to the Revolutionary Council in January 1986 were women.'[48] As one enthusiastic teenage girl said to me at a PDPA rally in Kabul in early 1989: 'This revolution was made for women!'

In 1986 the DOAW was renamed All-Afghan Women's Council, and also underwent a shift in orientation. It became less radical and more of a service organization providing social and legal services to poor Afghan women. During the late 1980s the Women's Council was led by Massouma Esmaty Wardak, an early DOAW member and member of parliament, but not a PDPA member.[49]

The early PDPA's emphasis on the 'Woman Question' subsided in favour of a concerted effort at 'national reconciliation', which began in January 1987. In the constitution of November 1988, the result of a *Loya Jirga*, or traditional assembly, PDPA members and activists from the Women's Council tried to retain an article stipulating the equality of women with men. However, this was opposed by the non-PDPA members of the assembly.

A compromise was reached in the form of another article, which stated that all Afghan citizens, male and female, have equal rights and obligations before the law.[50] This is article 38, which stated:

Citizens of the Republic of Afghanistan — men and women — have equal rights and duties before the law, irrespective of national, racial, linguistic, tribal, educational and social status, religion, creed, political conviction, occupation, kinship, wealth, and residence. The designation of any illegal privilege of discrimination against rights and duties of citizens is forbidden.

Women in Kabul and in Peshawar: a comparison

DURING the 1980s in areas under government control, and especially in Kabul, women were present in the different ranks of the party and the government, with the exception of the Council of Ministers. The *Loya Jirga* included women delegates; in 1989 the Parliament had seven female members. In 1989, women in prominent positions included Massouma Esmaty Wardak, president of the Women's Council; Shafiqeh Razmandeh, vice-president of the Women's Council; Soraya, director of the Afghan Red Crescent (Red Cross) Society; Zahereh Dadmal, director of the Kabul Women's Club; Dr Soheila, chief surgeon of the Military Hospital, who also held the rank of general. The Central Committee of the PDPA had several women members, including Jamila Palwasha and Ruhafza (alternate member), a working-class grandmother and 'model worker' at the Kabul Construction Plant (where she did electrical wiring).

In Kabul in January and February 1989, I saw women employees in all the government agencies and social organizations I visited. Ariana Airlines employed female as well as male flight attendants. An employee of the Peace, Solidarity and Friendship Organization told me that he was 37 and a man, yet had a supervisor who was 10 years his junior and a woman. There were women radio announcers, and the evening news on television (whether in Pushtu or Dari) was read by one male and one unveiled female announcer. There were women technicians as well as reporters working for radio and television, and in the country's newspapers and magazines. Women workers were present in the binding section of a printing house in Kabul; in the page-setting section of the Higher and Vocational Education press house; at the state-run CREPCA carpet company (where young women wove carpets and received a wage); and at the Kabul Construction Plant (which specialized in housing and pre-fabricated materials).

Like their male counterparts, these women were members of the Central Trade Union. I also saw one woman employee (and several women volunteer soldiers) at Pol-e Charkhi prison; she was assigned to the women's section where she oversaw the six remaining female political prisoners, all charged with terrorist acts. I was told that there were women soldiers and officers in the regular armed forces, as well as in the militia and Women's Self Defence (Defence of the Revolution) Units. There were women in security, intelligence, and the police agencies, women involved in logistics in the Defence Ministry,

women parachutists and even women veterinarians — an occupation usually
off-limits to women in Islamic countries. In 1989, all female members of the
PDPA received military training and arms. These women were prominent at a
party rally of some 50,000 held in Kabul in early February 1989.

Above the primary level, schools were now segregated, and middle
school and secondary school girls were taught by female teachers — this was
a concession made to traditionalist elements. In offices and other workplaces,
however, there was no segregation. Neither were buses divided into male and
female sections.

During the 1980s, a number of social organizations had considerable
female participation and visibility. Apart from the PDPA itself, they included
the Council of Trade Unions, the Democratic Youth Organization, the Peace,
Solidarity and Friendship Organization, the Women's Council, and the Red
Crescent Society. Two of these organizations were led by women: the president
of the Afghan Red Crescent Society was Soraya (no last name), and the Afghan
Women's Council also had female leadership. In the late 1980s the Afghan
Women's Council (AWC) was run by Massouma Esmaty Wardak and her staff
of eight women.[51] Although, as we have noted, Wardak was not a PDPA
member, some of her staff were. She is a graduate of the Academy of Sciences
with a degree in sociology and an interest in literature and history. Among her
published works is a book, *The Position and Role of Afghan Women in Afghan
Society: From the Late 18th to the Late 19th Century*. She also wrote the
introduction to a book on Mahmud Tarzi.

In discussions with Wardak and Soraya, I learnt that the Women's
Council was less political and more social and service-oriented than in the past.
The AWC provided social services to women, such as literacy and vocational
training in such fields as secretarial work, hairdressing, and sewing (workshops
were located in the complex); organized income-generating activities such as
handicraft production (mainly rugs and carpets, as well as sewing); offered
assistance to mothers and widows of 'martyrs of the Revolution' in the form of
pensions and coupons; and gave legal advice, mainly through a network of
women lawyers. Some women had 'outwork' arrangements with the AWC, as
Esmaty Wardak explained to me: 'They prefer to work at home; they bring their
work to us and we pay them.' During two trips to the Women's Council, I was
able to observe dozens of women (many of them poor and veiled) entering the
grounds to attend a class or to seek advice.

Wardak told me that the AWC had a membership of 150,000 with

branches in all provinces bar two. The branches organized traditional festivals
that included awards for handicraft pieces, and 'peace camps' which provided
medical care and distributed garments and relief goods free of charge. The
branches also assisted women in income-generating activities, such as raising
chickens and producing eggs and milk for sale, as well as sewing and craftwork.
The work of the AWC was supported by the government, which provided it with
a generous budget.[52]

The principal objectives of the AWC, according to its president, were to
raise women's social consciousness, to make them aware of their rights,
particularly their right to literacy and work, and to improve women's living
conditions and professional skills. She stressed equal pay with men and
workplace childcare as two important achievements. There was also an ongoing
radio and TV campaign against 'the buying and selling of girls', which still
continued. In early 1989, the AWC was also trying to change the laws on child
custody that favour the father and his agnates.

Like the AWC, the Kabul Women's Club was located in spacious
grounds, held two-hour literacy classes daily, conducted vocational training,
and housed employment workshops where women wove rugs and carpets,
sewed uniforms, embroidered, and produced handicrafts. The work was entirely
waged, and childcare and transportation were provided. Courses on home
management, health, hairdressing, and typing were offered free of charge. The
Women's Club also worked with the Public Health Ministry on mother-and-
child issues, such as the prevention of diseases, vaccination of children, breast-
feeding, and family planning.[53]

In Kabul I asked many party members, and workers of the Afghan
Women's Council, if women's rights would be sacrificed on the altar of national
reconciliation. All were fervent believers in the party's duty to defend the gains
made in women's rights, and in the ability of the women's organizations to stand
up for women's rights to education and employment. Among women in the
capital, there was considerable hostility toward the *mujahidin*, and I was told
several times that 'the women would not allow' a *mujahidin* takeover.

In Peshawar the situation of women and the opportunities afforded them
were very different. Unlike liberation, resistance, and guerrilla movements
elsewhere, the Afghan *mujahidin* never encouraged the active participation of
women. In Cuba, Algeria, Vietnam, China, Eritrea, Oman, Iran, Nicaragua, El
Salvador, and Palestine, women were/are active in the front lines, in party
politics, and in social services. It is noteworthy that the *mujahidin* had no female

spokespersons. Indeed, women in Peshawar who became too visible or vocal were threatened and sometimes killed. The group responsible for most of the intimidation of women was the fundamentalist *Hizb-e Islami*, led by Gulbeddin Hekmatyar who, over the years, received substantial military, political, and financial support from the United States, Pakistan, and Saudi Arabia.

The education situation in Peshawar was extremely biased against girls. In 1988, some 104,600 boys were enrolled in schools as against 7,800 girls. For boys there were 486 primary schools, 161 middle schools and four high schools. For girls there were 76 primary schools, two middle schools, and no high schools.[54] A UNICEF study indicated that there were only 180 Afghan women with a high school education in the camps.

The subordinate status of women was apparently decried by some in Peshawar. The Revolutionary Association of Women of Afghanistan (RAWA) was founded in 1977 (as a Maoist group) but became prominent on 4 February 1987 when its founder, Mina Kishwar Kamal, was killed by Islamists in Quetta. RAWA staged a demonstration by women and children in Rawalpindi on 27 December 1988 on the occasion of the ninth anniversary of the Soviet military intervention in Afghanistan. The demonstrators distributed pamphlets that attacked, in the strongest terms, the KGB, *Khad* (the Afghan political police), and the *Hizb-e Islami*. They claimed that the majority of Afghans stood for an independent and democratic Afghanistan, where social justice and freedom to women were guaranteed.[55] In a communiqué distributed that day, RAWA deplored: 'The reactionary fanatics [who] are savagely suppressing our grieved people, specially [sic] the women.' It continued:

> Killing the innocent men and women, raping, to marry forcefully young girls and widows, and hostility toward women [sic] literacy and education, are some customary cruelties committed by the fundamentalists who have made the life inside and outside the country bitter and suffocating. In their cheap opinion, the women struggle for any right and freedom is regarded as infidelity which must be suppressed brutaly [sic].

The communiqué decried the 'anti-democratic, anti-woman' activities of the fundamentalists and warned of 'fundamentalist fascism' replacing the Najibullah regime.

Following the withdrawal of Soviet troops in February 1989, there was some hope that a compromise could be reached between the government of

President Najibullah and the *mujahidin*. To facilitate this, the government revised its ideological and programmatic orientation. Following its congress in spring 1990, the PDPA changed its name to the *Hizb-e Watan*, or the Homeland Party. Constitutional changes were also made, stressing Islam and nation and dropping altogether references to the equality of men and women. Clearly, a decision had been made that the emancipation of women would have to await peace, stability, reconstruction, and development. But by April 1992, under pressure from the new UN Secretary-General, Boutros Boutros-Ghali, and his envoy, Benon Sevan, President Najibullah agreed to give up power. This triggered demoralization and desertion in the Afghan military, dissension within the government, and the takeover of Kabul by *mujahidin* fighters. Once they came to power, the *mujahidin* factions began to fight each other, but the men all agreed on the question of women. Thus the very first order of the new government was that all women should wear veils. As one journalist wrote from Kabul in early May 1992:

> The most visible sign of change on the streets, apart from the guns, is the utter disappearance of women in western clothes. They used to be a common sight. Now women cover up from ankle to throat and hide their hair, or else use the *burqa*. Many women are frightened to leave their homes. At the telephone office, 80 percent of the male workers reported for duty on Saturday, and only 20 percent of the females.[56]

Summary and conclusion

THIS chapter underscores the importance of the issue of women's rights in the Afghan revolution and civil conflict. To place the Marxist reform programme of 1978 in historical perspective, the struggle for women's rights has been surveyed from the earliest reforms in the nineteenth century to 1989. I have also described the patriarchal social structure to explain the necessity for the reforms as well as reaction to them. Like modernization itself, efforts to improve the status of women have been constrained by a social structure characterized by patriarchal gender relations, 'tribal feudalism', and a weak central state. Afghanistan is not the only patriarchal country, but it is an extreme case of 'classic patriarchy'. A rugged terrain and its armed tribes have combined to make modernization and centralization a difficult, prolonged, and limited enterprise, with serious, and dire, implications for the advancement of women.

This chapter has also highlighted parallels between the reforms of King Amanullah and those of the PDPA. In both cases, reforms threatened to upset the entire structure of patriarchal relations and property rights, thereby leading to rural resistance. As Charles Tilly has shown in his study of causes and forms of 'collective action', there is a pattern of reactionary movements by declining or threatened social classes. Contenders who are in danger of losing their place in a polity are especially prone to 'reactive' collective action, often taking communal forms, as was the case in Afghanistan.

There can be no doubt that the manner in which land reform and women's emancipation were implemented following the Saur Revolution was seriously flawed. Some of the audacious symbols of the revolution — red flags, the term comrade, pictures of Lenin and the like — were also ill-advised considering the extremely conservative and patriarchal social structure, and they contributed to the hostility. Nevertheless, the conflict in Afghanistan must be understood as a contest over two unalterably opposed political-cultural projects: development and reform on the one hand, tribal authority and patriarchal relations on the other.

It is remarkable that the subversion of a government which was undertaking wide-reaching and progressive social reforms, especially toward the emancipation of women, should have been encouraged (and financed) by the United States and China, both ostensibly committed to women's equality. But more dismaying has been the spectacle of Western intellectuals and leftists acting as cheerleaders for the *mujahidin*. Attempts to explain away the rather extreme forms of patriarchy existing among the *mujahidin* and in tribal communities by recourse to a vague cultural relativism are suspect.

For one thing, the cultural relativist argument pertaining to women has not been applied to neighbouring Iran, which has been judged by universal standards and norms. For another, there is nothing acceptable or 'natural' about ethnic, gender, or class oppression. It is entirely appropriate to interrogate cultural practices, political discourses, and social arrangements which occlude important questions about class, property, ethnicity, and gender. In particular, movements for national liberation must be judged on their social programme, especially on women's rights. If 'freedom', 'liberation' and 'autonomy' are goals for the nation, the community, and men only, then this is reason enough not to support a movement.[57]

Notes

1. Louis Dupree, *Afghanistan* (Princeton: Princeton University Press, 1980); Olivier Roy, *Islam and Resistance in Afghanistan* (Cambridge, UK: Cambridge University Press, 1990) (2nd edition).

2. Vartan Gregorian, *The Emergence of Modern Afghanistan* (Stanford: Stanford University Press, 1969); Thomas Hammond, *Red Flag Over Afghanistan* (Boulder, Colo: Westview, 1984), p. 5; Mark Urban, *War in Afghanistan* (New York: St Martin's Press, 1988), p. 204.

3. Gregory Massell, *The Surrogate Proletariat: Moslem Women and Revolutionary Strategies in Soviet Central Asia 1919-29* (Princeton, NJ: Princeton University Press, 1974), p. 9.

4. On Pushtunwali and Islam, see Olivier Roy, op. cit., pp. 34-7; John C Griffiths, *Afghanistan* (Boulder, Colo: Westview, 1981), pp. 111-12; Inger Boesen, 'Conflicts of Solidarity in Pukhtun Women's Lives', pp. 104-25 in Bo Utas (ed.) *Women in Islamic Society* (Copenhagen: Scandinavian Institute of Asian Studies, 1983).

5. On the brideprice and property rights, see Nancy Tapper, 'Causes and Consequences of the Abolition of Brideprice in Afghanistan', pp. 291-305 in M Nazif Shahrani and Robert L Canfield (eds.) *Revolutions and Rebellions in Afghanistan* (Berkeley, Calif: Institute of International Studies, 1984), and *Bartered Brides: Politics, Gender and Marriage in our Afghan Tribal Society* (Cambridge, UK: Cambridge University Press, 1991). A comprehensive study is in Mohammad Hashim Kamali, *Law in Afghanistan: A Study of the Constitutions, Matrimonial Law and the Judiciary* (Leiden: E J Brill, 1985). See also Raja Anwar, *The Tragedy of Afghanistan* (London: Verso, 1988), esp. Chapter 11, 'The Contradictions of Afghan Society'.

6. Haleh Afshar, 'The Position of Women in an Iranian Village', in H Afshar, (ed.) *Women, Work and Ideology in the Third World* (London: Tavistock, 1985), esp. pp. 75-6; Günseli Berik, *Women Carpet Weavers in Rural Turkey: Patterns of Employment, Earnings, and Status* (Geneva: ILO, 1987) esp. Ch. 4; Deniz Kandiyoti, 'Rural Transformation in Turkey and Its Implications for Women's Status', in UNESCO, *Women on the Move* (Paris, UNESCO, 1984), pp. 17-30.

7. John Caldwell, *A Theory of Fertility Decline* (New York: Academic Press, 1982); Deniz Kandiyoti, 'Bargaining with Patriarchy', *Gender and Society* 2 (3) (September, 1988), pp. 274-90.

8. On *fitna*, see Fatna Sabbah, *Woman in the Muslim Unconscious* (New York: Pergamon Press, 1984); Mai Ghoussoub, 'Feminism — or the Eternal Masculine — in the Arab World', *New Left Review* 161 (January/February 1987), pp. 3-13; Naila Kabeer, 'Subordination and Struggle: Women in Bangladesh', *New Left Review* 168 (March/April 1988), p.95.

9. The term 'culture against women' is from Hanna Papanek. See her essay, 'To Each Less Than She Needs, From Each More Than She Can Do: Allocations, Entitlements, and Values', pp. 162-181 in Irene Tinker, *Persistent Inequalities* (New York, Oxford: Oxford University Press, 1990). See also Valentine M Moghadam, 'Patriarchy and the Politics of Gender in Modernising Societies: Iran, Pakistan and Afghanistan', *International Sociology* 7 (1) (March 1992), pp. 35-53.

10. Tapper, 'The Abolition of Brideprice', p. 293. See also Tapper, *Bartered Brides*, pp. 45, 104, 142.

11. Griffiths, op. cit., p. 78.

12. See Tapper, op. cit., pp. 110-11. See also Boesen, op. cit., p. 107.

13. Hafizullah Emadi, 'State, Modernization and the Women's Movement in Afghanistan', *Review of Radical Political Economics* 23 (3&4) (1991), pp. 225-6. On gender stereotypes, see also Tapper, *Bartered Brides*, pp. 209-10.

14. Veronica Doubleday, *Three Women of Herat* (Austin: University of Texas Press, 1988), p. 149.

15. This was confirmed in interviews with Dr Saidali Jalali and Dr Azizullah Saidi, Indira Gandhi Hospital, Kabul, 11 February 1989. For data on health and other social indicators, see Valentine M Moghadam, *Modernizing Women: Gender and Social Change in the Middle East* (Boulder, Colo: Lynne Rienner Publishers, 1993), Chapter 7.

16. Boesen, op. cit.; Tapper, 'Abolition of the Brideprice'; Doubleday, op. cit.; Simone Bailleau Lajoinie, *Conditions de femmes en Afghanistan* (Paris: *Notre Temps/Monde*, 1980).

17. Massell, op. cit., pp. 160-163; Tapper, *Bartered Brides*, esp. Chapters 7, 8, 9.

18. For a thorough discussion of state capabilities, refer to Joel Migdal, *Strong Societies and Weak States: State-Society Relations and State Capabilities in the Third World* (Princeton: Princeton University Press, 1988). On the weak Afghan state, see Urban, *War in Afghanistan*, p. 4.

19. See in particular Gregorian, *The Emergence of Modern Afghanistan*. See also Griffiths, *Afghanistan*; Hammond, *Red Flag Over Afghanistan*, and Henry Bradsher, *Afghanistan and the Soviet Union* (Durham, NC: Duke University Press, 1985); Urban, op. cit.

20. Gregorian, op. cit., p. 3.

21. Urban, op. cit., p. 204.

22. Gregorian, op. cit., p. 309.

23. Ibid., p. 356.

24. Ibid., p. 309.

25. Ibid., p. 138. See also Lajoinie, op. cit., p. 61. This is known as the levirate.

26. Gregorian, op. cit., p. 139.

27. Ibid., p. 172.

28. Ibid., p. 198.

29. Ibid., p. 198.

30. Ibid., p. 241.

31. Ibid., p. 244.

32. Ibid., p. 244.

33. See Massell, op. cit., p. 219.

34. Gregorian, op. cit., p. 264.

35. Kamali, *Law in Afghanistan*, op. cit., pp. 86-7.

36. Interview with Soraya, a founding member of the DOAW and past president, Kabul, 6 February 1989 and Helsinki, 8 October 1990. Soraya identified three of the four women parliamentarians: Anahita Ratebzad, Massouma Esmaty Wardak and Mrs Saljugi.

37. Nancy Hatch Dupree, 'Revolutionary Rhetoric and Afghan Women', pp. 306-40 in Nazif Shahrani and Robert L Canfield (eds.) *Revolutions and Rebellions in Afghanistan*.

38. Hugh Beattie, 'Effects of the Saur Revolution in Nahrin', in Shahrani and Canfield (eds.) *Revolutions and Rebellions in Afghanistan*, p.186.

39. Quoted in Tapper, 'Abolition of Brideprice in Afghanistan', p. 294.

40. Beattie, op. cit.

41. Suzanne Jolicoeur Katsikas, *The Arc of Socialist Revolutions: Angola to Afghanistan* (Cambridge, Mass: Schenkman Publishing Co., 1982), p. 231.

42. Beattie, op. cit., p. 191.

43. See Dupree, op. cit.

44. See Anwar, *Revolutionary Afghanistan*, esp. Chapters 14 and 15.

45. Interview with Soraya, Kabul, 6 February 1989.

46. Quoted in Dupree, op. cit., p. 330.

47. The formal reinstatement of Muslim Family Law did not apply to party members. Interview with a PDPA official, New York, 28 October 1986.

48. Urban, op. cit., p. 209.

49. Interview with Massouma Esmaty Wardak, Kabul, 1 February 1989.

50. Interview with Farid Mazdak, PDPA official, Kabul, 9 February 1989.

51. In 1990, Mrs Wardak was made Minister of Education, where she remained until the collapse of the government in 1992.

52. Interview with Massouma Esmaty Wardak, Kabul, 24 January 1989.

53. Interview with Zahereh Dadmal, Kabul, 8 February 1989.

54. *New York Times*, 2 April 1988, p. A2.

55. Rahimullah Yusufzai, 'Afghanistan: Withdrawal Symptoms', *The Herald* (January, 1989).

56. Derek Brown, 'New Afghanistan Carries on Grisly Game of the Old', *The Guardian* (UK), 4 May 1992, p. 7.

57. On this point, see the debate in *Against the Current* No. 17 (November/December 1988, No. 19 (March/April 1989), and No. 20 (May/June 1989) around my position on Afghanistan.

Chapter 6

Modernity, Islamization, and women in Iran

Nayereh Tohidi

ONE fundamental challenge for global feminism is that the conception, objectives, and strategy of feminism in different nations and regions have become intertwined with very different economic, socio-cultural, and political conditions. Women's status and feminist demands in most of the Western advanced capitalist societies have been conceived in terms of four areas: economic autonomy, access to power and authority, a single uniform sexual standard for men and women, and the ending of invidious stereotypes of gender.[1] In a developing country like Iran, however, specific factors have shaped feminist consciousness differently. Consequently, women's demands have not been necessarily conceptualized in terms of those four areas.

Two historical and revolutionary developments in the West — that is, industrial capitalism and representative democracy — that played crucial roles in paving the way for the emergence of the women's movement and feminist consciousness, have never prevailed in Iran. Consequently, their important cultural and socio-psychological ramifications, namely, transformation of the structure and functions of the family; liberalization and secularization of the state, law and education; establishment of civil rights; respect for individual freedom; and appreciation of independence and individual autonomy have not been realized in Iranian society yet. It is true that it took years of fierce struggle on the part of Western women to succeed in extending the new democratic and civil rights to the female half of the population. But the very emergence and growing popularity of liberalism and the ideals of 'liberty, equality and fraternity' during the Enlightenment era, although originally meant for men, did serve women as a frame of reference, the very frame of reference that Iranian women have lacked.

This chapter examines the main historical, economic, political, cultural, and socio-psychological factors that have shaped the 'Woman Question' and the feminist movement in the Iranian context. I intend to show how the objectives of nation-building, national identity, strategies of socio-economic development, and modernization have been interwoven with the 'Woman Question'. I also hope to show that rather than Islamic doctrine *per se*, certain historical, political, and economic factors (both endogenous and exogenous), as well as cultural, ideological, and socio-psychological dimensions have interactively contributed to the recent revival of patriarchal Islamist fervour.

Historical specificities

THE Constitutional Revolution (1906-1911) in Iran possessed a bourgeois democratic character only in a limited sense, as was the case with the Turkish revolution of 1908 and the Chinese revolution of 1911. Despite its progressive and revolutionary objectives, many of which were similar to those of the European and American revolutions, the Constitutional Movement failed to transform economic and political foundations of the society. The weakness of the bourgeoisie in tackling the basis of the patrimonial semi-feudal power structure; its lack of decisiveness in facing interference by British and Tsarist Russia; the absence of a properly formed working class;[2] and uncertainty, or the lack of consensus, among the intellectuals over what constituted modernization, were among the major factors responsible for the inability of the Constitutional Movement to reach its goals.

The Constitutional Movement failed to replace monarchic despotism with a constitutional representative democracy. Nor did the Movement succeed in secularization and laicization of the state and the law. The Islamist clergy retained their influence over the state. Despite their unprecedented participation in the Movement, women's suffrage was not even raised as an issue.[3] Women were still fighting for more basic rights such as access to education. But the Constitutional Movement was not totally fruitless for women. The spread of progressive ideas influenced people's attitudes. Women's participation in the Movement was followed by the establishment of consciousness-raising associations and women's publications.

The first school for Muslim girls, Namus, which was founded in 1907, was quickly followed by several others during those revolutionary years.

However, all were funded by private money, clearly indicating no central endorsement.

Another failure of the Constitutional Movement that had significant ramifications for the 'Woman Question' was its inability to rid the country of neo-colonial penetration. As a result, semi-colonial obstacles hindered economic growth based on the local capitalist accumulation and the dynamism of the industrial sector. This is due to the fact that the development of a dynamic domestic sector capable of generating self-sustained growth and domestic decision-making centres had been prevented.

Forty years later, between 1951 and 1953, Iranian nationalists and progressive forces mobilized people once more in an attempt to democratize the society, develop the economy, and strengthen the national industries. Led by the National Front and Mohammad Mossadeq, the Prime Minister, and with massive participation of the people, including women, the movement sought nationalization of the oil industry (then under British control), restriction of the monarch's power, establishment of the rule of law, and enforcement of the constitution and the parliament. However, an American-supported (CIA) coup against Mossadeq returned all power to the Shah, ending this last promising attempt by Iranian democratic forces with another defeat. Now the conditions had been set for what Hamza Alavi has called a typical 'neo-colonial mode of production'.[4]

Despite the increasing economic penetration and political influence of the West, Iran has been the product of a dialectic, a synthesis, not just a simple imposition, in which the social institutions and cultural values of the West (imperialistic or otherwise) form one of the terms of the dialectic, as Worsley notes.[5] A blend of native culture (Iranian nationalism), Islam, and Westernism has moulded the contemporary identity of Iran. Since the Constitutional Movement of 1906-11, any major political and ideological discourse, including the 'Woman Question', has been fought out in an uneasy triangle involving Islam, Westernism and nationalism.

In modern Iran, as in many other developing countries, the gap between infrastructure and superstructure has increasingly widened. Culture, value systems, and attitudes have lagged drastically behind the abrupt economic and material transitions. Structural incoherence has widened the gap between 'modern' and 'traditional' sectors in all fields and aspects of society. But this has not been simply a problem of 'tradition versus modernity', as some analysts have suggested. The problem lies in the way modernity and modernization have been introduced and implemented in the Iranian society. Although the influence and penetration of Western advanced capitalism speeded up certain dimensions of technological and industrial capitalistic development in Iran, the totality of social transformation (that is, modernization), was impeded. In his socio-psychological analysis of human relations in contemporary Islamic societies of the Near East, Halpern argues that:

> Imperialism kept all transformers out of power and deliberately inhibited their work for at least the first half of the twentieth century. The first generation of local ruling élites — and usually not only the first — often confused a falsely vivified Westernization with the genuine and world-wide movement of modernization.[6]

Iran's modernization has not been all-encompassing, affecting every dimension of society. Industrialization, economic transformation, political development, and cultural and ideological changes have not followed each other persistently and coherently. Halpern states that 'modernization is the overcoming of persistent *incoherence* through persistent transformation'. In Iran, however, the absence of a domestically led self-sustained dynamism for modernization, lack of a national-oriented strategy for economic development, and the elimination of advocates who could enlist full social capacity in the service of transformation have allowed incoherence to become a persistent anomaly of the 'modern' society. It is not that people in other societies can avoid incoherence in the modern age, but rather that, for the majority of Iranians, 'incoherence breaks out again and again in unintended, uncontrolled ways, and not primarily through the conscious, creative breaking of crippling relationships'.[7] For example, it takes more than the unveiling of women (let alone the coercive unveiling from above by the government and police interference as was the case in 1936 Iran), to modernize women's role and to overcome the crippling patriarchal relationship in the Muslim family. Radical change in one aspect of society without corresponding changes in other domains only intensifies incoherence and introduces new conflicts and contradictions.

While modernism within Western culture arose mainly through discovery and invention, the basic process causing abrupt changes in Iranian culture was diffusion. Certain exploitative characteristics of this process of one-way diffusion culminated in resentment and rejection on the part of Iranian men and women who perceived modernization as simply imperialism in disguise. Those characteristics included: a drastic and widening urban-rural gap; a growing maldistribution of wealth and acute class polarization; a too heavy reliance on a single product, that is, petroleum, and specialization in only raw materials increasing political repression and bureaucratic corruption; and a societal disintegration and cultural lag.[8] In other words, the capitalist development and industrialization in Iran underwent an 'abnormal' dwarf-like formation, creating an uneven economy and what Cardoso and Faletto called 'structural dualism'.[9] The process of modernization generally became one of emulating as many as possible of the outward features of the Western societies, particularly with regard to consumption patterns. As noted by Bill and Leiden: 'Discotheques and mosques, modern luxury hotels and squalid mud huts, nuclear energy programmes and the fuel of animal droppings, F-16s and old rifles and daggers, palaces and tents, computerized libraries and omnipresent illiteracy',[10] as well as the miniskirt and the *chador* (the traditional veil), exemplified the bizarre duality, incoherence, and inequality in every dimension of pre-revolutionary Iran.

Women, development, and modernization in Iran

IN Iran, as elsewhere, the impact of capitalist development has been so different for men and women that the changes for women require separate study from those of men. However, Middle East women's studies, including that of Iran, has remained relatively isolated from the theoretical issues fought over in women-in-development literature. This is due, in part, to the fact that in comparison with other areas in the Third World, multinational corporations have had a much less direct impact on the lives of Middle Eastern women. Moreover, certain problems present in the study of the Middle East, for example, 'orientalism' and 'essentialism', have limited most studies on women in the Middle East toward the sexual ideology of Islam, the question of the veil, and sex segregation.[11] It is only recently that the study of Middle Eastern women is taking as its point of reference the study of women 'in relationship to the internal dynamics of the historical moment, as opposed to the reified and static conceptualizations of Islam and the family'.[12]

The women-in-development literature has demonstrated that the usually male-oriented economic development and the promotion of industry and cash crops have led to economic regression for women.[13] This has been confirmed also in the case of Iran, especially in rural areas.[14] In her 1965-76 study in the tribal area of Boir Ahmad, south-west Iran, Friedl showed that modernization and economic development restricted women's options more than the traditional cultural-economic frame had done. Village women, once producers of surplus in the local economy, became 'consumers inspired by an urban lifestyle and dependent on sources of income removed from the village and largely beyond their control'.[15]

Although this chapter critically assesses the impact of modernization on Iranian women, I do not mean to suggest that industrialization and capitalist development are to be blamed as the causes of the existing gender disparity and oppression of women in Iran. On the contrary, it seems that a completely successful bourgeois-democratic revolution, during the 1906-11 Constitutional Movement, entailing industrialization, economic advancement, and political development could have democratized and secularized the then semi-feudal society of Iran. Such transformations could have led to access to secular education, women's wage employment and economic autonomy, political and social sophistication of women, individuation, and eradication of suffocating patrimonial familial traditions, all paving the way for women's emancipation, as several scholars have argued.[16]

When viewed from a comparative perspective, industrialization and certain bourgeois transformations seem to be inevitable processes for the national and political development of Iran, the progress of the women's movement, and the feasibility of socialistic alternatives. It seems that in some European societies (especially Scandinavia) many of the adverse and regressive ramifications of capitalism on women's position have been short-lived. Women's own collective and conscious efforts along with social-democratic reforms have actually reversed some of those adverse trends, enabling women to enjoy (relative to the present world standards) a high status and a high level of well-being. It is clear that women's own collective action and conscious participation are critical in the materializing of political achievements for women in any modern economic system.

The inherent tendency of capital to seize upon existing divisions, inequalities, and hierarchies (such as gender and racial inequalities) in order to intensify exploitation and increase management control can be partly countered only by people's conscious and organized resistance. In Iran, due to a repressive political system, however, such collective and conscious participation of people, particularly women, in the process of development has been prevented. As in many other Third World countries, Iranian women have not been integrated in development plans, or, when they have, it has not always been to their advantage. Many adverse effects of development on Iranian women or men have stemmed from its distorted character, rather than from its merely capitalistic nature. An imbalanced modernization and the underdeveloped character of Iranian capitalism — partial industrialization, structural duality (articulation of some elements of a capitalist system and pre-capitalist modes of production), imperialistic and external orientation of most of the development projects — have had serious ramifications for people's economic, cultural and psychological well-being. The following pages focus on the effects of modernization on rural and urban women in Iran, in order to provide an explanatory background to the appeal of Islamism.

Rural women

AS has been demonstrated for Latin America,[17] and in Iran, partial industrialization dislodged workers from agriculture faster than they could be absorbed into industry. Based on the traditional model of development, men were the primary target of absorption into industry. Therefore, in spite of new job opportunities and the generation of income for a limited number of urban women, the overall daily life and economic position of the majority of women declined. It seems that changes in rural areas, growing urbanization, and rural to urban migration in recent decades have increased Iranian women's economic dependence on men.

In the first stage of the Iranian land reform programme (1961-63), the majority of peasants received very small, fragmented plots of land and lacked appropriate technology and financial means to afford machinery. Their reliance on intensive family labour consequently increased. Partial mechanization of labour, whenever available, often occurred in the share of the work traditionally assigned to male peasants, thereby increasing rather than reducing the women's work. For instance, better ploughed and irrigated land needs more frequent weeding, the task traditionally assigned to women in the peasant division of labour.[18] Some studies on women's specific role in post-revolutionary Iran's rural economy document the same pattern. That is, women's labour contribution to both agricultural production and the income generated from the produce is much greater than that of men. Hossein Nayer's study of a village in Khorasan, north-east Iran, shows that women's share in production comprises 68 per cent of the entire agricultural and pastoral work against 32 per cent of men's. The monetary output of women's work is more than twice that of men's (40 million against 19 million Rials).[19]

Moreover, the inefficiency of small plots of land and the increasing need for cash income forced large numbers of men to migrate to the cities in search of a job in construction or industry, leaving most of the agricultural work and the household responsibilities entirely to women. In the case of large-scale commercialization and mechanization of land allocated for growing cash crops for exports, the tradition has been to employ men as seasonal farm labourers thus depriving women of paid agricultural work. The growth of the market for Iranian carpets led to a great increase in the number of carpet weavers, 90 per cent of whom are rural women; 40 per cent of them below the age of fifteen. [20] But growth in this field has not helped rural women's economic position, either because the majority of rural carpet weavers are unpaid family workers or because their payments are under the control of male kin.

In short, the 'modernization' measures implemented in rural areas failed to improve rural women's status in Iran. Increasing economic dependence on men reinforced the traditional emphasis on early marriage for women and their primary role as the bearers of sons. The illiteracy rate among rural women remained as high as 83 per cent (according to the 1976 census). In her study on the daily life of the settled tribal women of Mamasani in southern Iran, Shahshahani observes that rural changes brought about through development have undermined the reciprocal economic ties and obligations in the rural family, including the balance between husbands and wives in terms of workload and labour productivity. This finding confirms Boserup's central point in her study of women in rural development: whenever commercialized and mechanized labour-saving techniques have been made available, women's work has been displaced by men's role in production.

Following men's migration, women were frequently pressed to abandon their village because of the heavy labour needed to farm and the agricultural inefficiency of their small plots. These newly migrated men and women, who usually ended up as seasonal labourers, peddlers, or small traders residing in slums, turned out to be one of the first militant groups of the masses who joined the traditional middle-class supporters of Khomeini in the anti-Shah movement. Most of the recent female migrants to the metropolitan centres like Tehran found themselves relegated to the limited role of a housewife with no reliable productive role, with increased economic dependence on men, and with restricted social conditions.

In her study of female migrants in southern Tehran, Janet Bauer showed that following migration to the city, women were cut off from their previous social contacts and supportive kinship network. While experiencing marginality and insecurity, they had to deal with the additional pressures of such new requirements of urban life as the modernizing pressure of consumption. She observed that improvement in the economic status of the husbands of these new migrants was coupled with women's intensified subordination, restrictions, domesticity, and isolation. It was precisely for such women that mosques and religious rites and rituals offered a much needed opportunity to assemble.[21] In her study on traditional women in Shiraz, central Iran, Ann Betteridge pointed to similar reasons behind women turning to mosques and their proliferation of religious activities in the years preceding the 1978-79 revolution.[22]

Urban women

DURING the 1970s, the cities were the centre of the most drastic changes and visible social-political upheaval, while peasants and the rural population remained largely separate from the movement. This may signify the importance of socio-psychological factors during rapid modernization: newly urbanized women and men experienced 'relative deprivation' due to their exposure to new possibilities, in which they expected a share but which the system could not provide. Literacy and education increased people's aspirations, but political repression, fierce economic competition, the conflict-ridden and stressful lifestyle of big cities resulted in incoherence, frustration, and anomie.

The impact of modernization on the strata of women who had been urbanized for several generations had somewhat different ramifications. During the decade preceding the 1979 revolution, a significant number of urban women made impressive strides in education. In 1976, 43.5 per cent of urban women (compared to 6.6 per cent of rural women) were able to read and write. Women's college enrolment from 1971 to 1978 increased to 79 per cent (76 per cent for men).[23] The percentage of literate women among those employed increased from 30 per cent in 1966 to 65 per cent in 1976. Employed women with a bachelor's or higher degree increased from 17,000 to 109,000.[24]

Female participation in the measured labour force reached 11 per cent, which is high relative to the Middle Eastern standards of the time. During the same decade, job opportunities for women grew very slowly in industry (140,000 to 142,000) but showed much greater increase in the service sector (54,000 to 224,000); in technical and professional fields such as nursing, medicine, pharmacy, and in academia (48,000 to 170,000); and in teaching, secretarial and clerical work (14,000 to 198,000). All these changes culminated in a still small yet growing layer of very visible, unveiled, vocal, and educated women with an access to cash and a potential for financial autonomy.

This pattern of change contributed to an unprecedented physical and social presence of women in the public sphere of the modern cities of Iran. Their presence influenced women's expectations in general and their perception of gender roles in particular, threatening the traditional Muslim family structure and male domination. In addition to this threat to a culture that viewed women's role as centred around marriage and motherhood was a demographic change which increased the proportion of youths, and a rise in the age of marriage. The result was an unprecedented increase in the number of young, single women. This was seen as an especially threatening development since these young, single women were increasingly emulating the Western style of life. Their unveiledness, clothing styles, and public interactions with men — in total contradiction with the patriarchal notions of honour and virginity — were perceived by the Muslim mentality as necessarily linked with *fitna*, that is, social and moral disorder.[25]

Women's visibility came to be opposed by men, but it was also resented by many women. For the cultural lag, structural duality, and incoherence which resulted from the modernization process had affected women's lives as well. As economic class polarity widened among women, so did polarity between modern and traditional lifestyles. Among the urban middle class, two layers of women emerged, representing two distinctly different subcultures: *chadori* (veiled) women, representing the female folk of bazaar-oriented (merchants, traders, artisans, shopkeepers), traditional and religious petty bourgeoisie who were basically domesticated homemakers (housewives); and *beechador* (unveiled) women, representing modernized, educated females of the newly emerging *edaari*, that is, office-oriented (professionals, technicians, government employees), modern petty bourgeoisie who either worked outside the home or aspired to employment.

Whereas the economic interests, ideological stance and cultural traditions of the first group of women had been jeopardized and disrupted by the expansion of capitalism and modernization, the second group was actually the very product of the modernization process. Therefore, a process of conflict and friction set in between the growing, modernized group of men and women who embraced a Western-inspired lifestyle and found socio-cultural transformation to their advantage, and the large, traditional strata of women and men whose lifestyle, religious beliefs and cultural identity were being challenged and humiliated by the state's modernization measures.

Women and Islamic fundamentalism

ALTHOUGH modernization resulted in an increase in urban women's access to education and employment, enhancing their potential for self-empowerment and emancipation, the existing structural problems in the character of modernization led the majority of modernized women, as well as men, into an alienating, frustrating, and confusing state. Consequently, and contrary to a widely held assumption about women as mere victims or passive followers of Islamic fundamentalism, certain strata of women actually played an active and important role in the Islamic movement in general, and the articulation of the 'model of Islamic women' in particular.

Whereas the traditional woman's image was being increasingly portrayed as old-fashioned, ignorant and irrelevant, the modern woman's image on the other hand was soon considered to be 'Westoxicated' (meaning to be under the influence of the toxic culture of the West), objectified, and identity-less (*beehoviyyat*). During the 1960s and 1970s, it was precisely the traditional strata of women (and men), particularly the better educated, younger generation who constituted the principal economic and ideological constituency of Islamic fundamentalism in Iran. The younger generation of women from these strata experienced the crisis milieu, including the identity crisis of that historical juncture, most acutely. As the first generation from the traditional families, these younger women were being exposed to a high level of public education, a dramatically different set of ideas and values, and an occasional chance of a teaching career. Subsequently, with regard to women's role, they were soon caught up in the midst of a double bind, two conflicting and competing role models.[26] One was the traditional role reinforced by their families and the religious standards prescribing marriage, motherhood, and domestic functions. But this role was now regarded as old-fashioned and was losing its status for the more educated younger generation of the traditional middle class. The other role, that is, the modern image of womanhood, was seen as a Western import sanctioned by the Shah, the following of which implied complicity with Western intruders, nonconformity to Islamic mores, and thus a susceptibility to 'Westoxication'. Aside from its morally and politically negative implications, the modern Westernized role had yet to be proven as emancipatory. Among the concerns that undermined the desirability of the modern style of womanhood were low pay and fierce competition, limited access to higher education, limited options for decent jobs, sex discrimination and sexual harassment in the work place, too much stress and role strain due to the high expense or scarcity of quality child care and the problem of the 'double day', and a higher rate of marital conflicts and divorce among career women (in a culture where divorce was still frowned upon).

The younger educated female members of the traditional strata found neither of those roles attractive. Caught in a dilemma, these women began to seek an alternative role model. While exploring new sources of identity, self-worth, and purpose for women, they turned to the opposition forces and intellectuals such as Al-e Ahmed and Ali Shariati. Their passionate call for a 'return to the roots'; 'reaffirmation of the indigenous and authentic culture'; 'reappropriation of traditional values'; and revival or reconstruction of female images of the Islamic legends, like Fatimeh and Zeinab, in a politically more compatible character — that is, non-domesticated, non-passive, socially engaged, and politically militant — proved quite compelling.[27]

These anti-West sentiments and attitudes found their best reflection and articulation in a book called *Gharbzadegi* (West-struckness or Westoxication) written in 1964 by Jalal Al-e Ahmad, the most prominent and popular writer of the time. The writings of Al-e Ahmad, a leftist populist, along with the provocative lectures and essays of Ali Shariati, a French-educated Islamist reformist, played a critical role in the articulation and popularization of the 'anti-imperialist, anti-Westoxication' discourse of the 1978-79 revolution. Both of them identified the ongoing modernization process as imperialistic, exploitative, and toxic. Al-e Ahmad compared Westoxication to a disease (cholera) that had afflicted people's minds and hearts, usurping the nation's natural resources (particularly the oil), distorting people's identity and culture, and degenerating the entire moral fabric of the society. The 'Westoxicated woman' was now regarded as a primary vehicle through which imperialism succeeded in the implementation of its plots. Thus, a campaign against the 'Westoxicated woman' became one of the significant components of this ideological and political discourse. Muslim women writers and intellectuals, among them Fereshteh Hashemi, Zahra Rahnavard, and Tahereh Saffar Zadeh, joined Islamic revivalists in denouncing Westernized women, further articulating and reconstructing the Islamic model of womanhood.[28]

Women students who sought salvation in the new Islamic movement adopted an alternative style of clothing called *hijab-e Islami* (Islamic cover), which consisted of a scarf covering the hair, a tunic over a long-sleeved shirt, loose pants (or stockings) and flat shoes — all in a dark or neutral colour. This style of clothing, they argued, was neither so restrictive and traditional-looking as the *chador*, nor as exposing and objectifying as Western dress. It did not entail cosmetics and jewellery, thereby releasing women from excessive concern over looks, fashions, and consumerism. Moreover, they believed it could enhance uniformity and reduce competition over class disparities and physical appearance among female students, and provide an asexual and serious image appropriate for political activism. Psychologically, those women who felt inferior could compensate for it by claiming to be more virtuous and 'authentic' in comparison to modernized and affluent women. They used this puritanical model of womanhood as a culturally constituted defence mechanism against their own sexual impulses as well as men's sexual expectations.

As Baxter observes in the case of the Palestinian women's Islamic groups, this model provided women with a legitimate channel for social contact and participation in the public sphere.[29] It also offered them a simple and straightforward guideline for proper behaviour. Especially for adolescents living in a time of cultural uncertainty and social complexity, and at the stage of personality development in which the quest for identity is the central psychological issue,[30] this Islamic model served as both a reassuring and anxiety-reducing mechanism. In a sense, this was a puritanical attempt by educated reformist women to restore an Islamic identity distinct from the

'Westoxicated, commoditized' women. Their initial intention, therefore, and that of ideologues like Shariati who advocated an Islamic model for women, was not a 'return to the veil' or to the traditional domestic role. For instance, Shariati's own wife was an educated unveiled woman and Al-e Ahmed's wife, Simin Daneshvar, was (and still is) a prominent writer, university lecturer, and an unveiled woman, more progressive than her husband. Shariati, while being disliked by most of the clergy for his implicit renunciation of their conservatism and reactionary interpretation of the Quran, including their backward views on women, was very popular among the younger, educated generation of women and men. However, when the anti-Shah movement, influenced by both the secular left and reformist Islamists as well as the Islamic fundamentalists, reached its upheaval, it was in the absence of people like Shariati and Al-e Ahmad (who had died earlier) that Khomeini emerged as the most influential opposition figure.

The clergy skilfully manipulated the revival of Islamic ideals and emotions toward a fundamentalistic and sectarian direction superseding the initial reformistic discourses of Islamists like Shariati and the *Mojahedin* organization.[31] As a result, the clerical leadership as well as Islamic women activists gradually enforced the adoption of the traditional veil (*chador*) as the most appropriate and politically strongest statement during the anti-Shah demonstrations. The notion of *gharbzadegi* served to politicize the veil, to convince some women and to intimidate many others that a refusal to wear the veil was not only un-Islamic but actually signified complicity with the Shah and the Western imperialists.

It should be noted that despite frictions and conflicts between the two layers of the middle-class women described above, many modern, unveiled, career-oriented women took part in the anti-Shah movement not in opposition to modernization or Westernization as such, but against the repressive dictatorship, exploitative influence of the West, extremely uneven distribution of the wealth, shallowness of women's emancipation, and bureaucratic corruption in their work places. However, the political naiveté of these women, and the absence of a democratic, secular, and progressive leadership, as well as ambiguity in the political discourses of the Islamic forces and the misleading promises of Khomeini, led almost all segments of the Shah's opposition to unite behind Khomeini, who was perceived then as a unifying spiritual figure.

Politics of the veil

THE phenomenon of the 'Westoxicated woman' (*zan-e gharbzadeh*) was seen as a major agent of 'cultural imperialism' contributing to the moral and cultural degeneration of Iranian society. Religious leaders, 'unable to speak openly, used women and sexual imagery as metaphors to discuss the dangers of imperialism and Westernization'.[32] The Westoxicated woman was culturally constructed as a negative image of the modern-minded woman. The stereotype was of a middle-class unveiled and Westernized woman without productive contributions or reproductive responsibilities. If she worked at all, it was as a secretary in private or public offices of the service sector, and her work was viewed mainly as decorative and dispensable. Her access to money was considered a waste, because it was used to cover the cost of her own clothing, cosmetics, and imported consumer goods. She was preoccupied with her physical appearance and European fashions, would wear mini-skirts, excessive make-up, mingle freely with men, smoke, drink, and laugh in public. She would read romantic novels, if she read at all, and pick her role models from among Hollywood stars, American soap operas, and pop singers. Her light-headedness and lack of interest in politics and national issues had made her easy prey for commercialization and toxication by the West, according to the stereotype. Ironically, many aspects of this characterization of Western women have been among the very traits that Western feminists have rejected as by-products of women's objectification in patriarchal capitalism. But in that historical context of Iran, such characterization was so predominant that any non-traditional unveiled woman was perceived as vulnerable to 'Westoxication'.

The motive behind this opposition to Westernized women was not limited to ideological, moral, and political reasons. A sense of competition between educated men and women in the new capitalist market made the modern women threatening.

An additional reason worthy of attention here is the history of unveiling in contemporary Iran. Similar to such traditions as footbinding in China, the veil in Iran has been used to define a woman's physical mobility/boundary in society. Kabeer shows that, in Pakistan and Bangladesh, the veil has limited women's presence and movement to only ten per cent of the available physical boundary of the society.[33] The veil has also signified the Muslim's perception of woman's sexuality as potentially subversive. It has reduced a woman's place and role to her sexual and reproductive dimensions. The veil has thus been a mechanism of patriarchal control, as well as a political device.

The subtle political function of the veil was unrecognized until 1934-36, however, when Reza Shah Pahlavi waged a forceful campaign against it. That campaign did not involve much education or consciousness-raising since women's emancipation was not the real motive — Reza Shah's drive for the mandatory unveiling of women was similar to that informing his simultaneous decree for changes in men's style of clothing. Inspired by modernization measures in Turkey under Kemal Ataturk, Reza Shah made several attempts to Europeanize Iranians' appearance. Men were ordered to shave their beards and adopt European styles of clothing — European hats, for example. Police were ordered to physically remove the *chador* from any woman wearing it in public. Women wearing *chador* or even *rousari* (headscarf) were not allowed to use any public facilities. Veiled women were harassed, humiliated, and chased by police and thugs. Even the costume of rural women, whenever it looked like the *chador*, was pulled away and torn down by the gendarmes.[34] This coercive method led to a backlash. Women who were unwilling or unable to abandon a norm to which they were so strongly accustomed resorted to staying behind closed doors to avoid embarrassing confrontation.

It is ironic that 40 years after Reza Shah's campaign, similar methods of violence, harassment, and humiliation were being used against women, but this time by the Islamic government to achieve veiling. If Reza Shah forced Iranian women to unveil themselves to appear Westernized, Khomeini forced them to veil themselves to appear anti-West! Reza Shah's campaign led to unveiling being identified with the repressive state and with Westernizing ambitions. This background was used by the fundamentalists to argue that the unveiling of Muslim women had been an imperialistic plot, thus propagating the veil as an effective weapon in the people's fight against the Shah and Western imperialists. This explains, in part, why the veil has become a central component of the political culture of the Islamic Republic as well as a major dimension of the identity of the model of Islamic womanhood. According to Islamic discourse, the re-adoption of *hijab* (the veil) has served to 'vaccinate' women and men against the virus of Westoxication. Several current slogans explicitly point to this underlying political function attributed by the Iranian

Islamists to *hijab*: 'My sister, your *hijab* is more combative than my blood'; 'your *hijab* turned into a fatal fire, burning the infidel enemy's heart'; and 'Islam is our ideology, *hijab* is our bastion'.

The politics of the veil in Iran and the role of the state, either the modernist anti-veil Pahlavi state or the present Islamic veil-advocated state, demonstrated that attempts to transform women's situation are least effective and most contradictory when implemented by force and from above with no conscious participation by the people. It is instructive that, just as the coercive and mandatory unveiling of the 1930s could not modernize Iranian women, neither could the violently imposed compulsory veiling of the 1980s succeed in turning women to seclusion or the limited officially prescribed boundaries. The present politicization of women, their rising consciousness and resilience, along with the material and economic imperatives of today's Iran, have kept women relatively active and visible in the social sphere far beyond the initial purpose of the veil and the traditional Islamic standards.

Women and national identity: a literary analysis

IN Iranian contemporary literature, there are frequent references to women's roles as purveyors of culture, guardians of tradition and pillars of national identity. In a 'patrimonial' political structure like that of Iran, the national system is often conceived in terms of the family metaphor.[35] This is yet another manifestation of the fact that, in Iran, as in many other colonized or neo-colonized countries, the 'Woman Question' has been tenaciously combined with the question of national identity, thus intertwining the liberation of women with national liberation and feminism with nationalism. This has further complic-ated the conceptualization of feminism and the course of women's emancipation in Iran.

Socio-economic transformations resulted in an interrogation of women's proper place and role. In this sense, Woman became a *question* to all: urban women, politicians, clerics, and the intelligentsia. During similar historical moments in the West, organized feminism (the women's rights movement and women's liberation movement) emerged as women's answer to that question.[36] In Iran, however, women were prevented from conceptualizing their own answer, developing their own movement and defining their own identity independent of the national movement and the question of national identity. In

Iran, as in the West, when an urban woman began working outside the home, especially when the work was not undertaken out of obvious economic necessity, she was immediately blamed for undermining or neglecting her natural and essential roles — that is, motherhood and wifehood. But in Iran, unlike the West, she also became liable to suffer Westoxication — a 'sin' unfamiliar to Western women. She could be accused of failing to safeguard the honour of the family and the cultural heritage of the country. A woman's failure to conform to the traditional norms could be labelled as renunciation of indigenous values and loss of cultural identity. She could be seen as complying with the forces of 'Western imperialists'. In short, women became hostage in the conflict between the security and legitimacy of tradition and the aspiration for full human dignity and liberation.[37]

Although this perception of modernized woman as liable to become involved in corruption and treason was common among traditional, fundamentalist religious segments, the secular nationalists, and even the Marxist left, were similarly suspicious of the modern middle-class woman. A modernized and employed woman had to prove that she had saved herself from the Western 'toxicating' influence. She had to prove her chastity (*nejabat*) and authenticity (*esalat*) to her potential husband. At the same time, in transactions with her male boss or male colleagues, she had to counter their sexual advances by proving that 'she was not that type'. In the anti-Shah, anti-imperialist movement, she had to prove her loyalty to the cause by postponing women's issues to the days after the revolution. While Marxist comrades supported public and emancipated roles for women, the Marxist Iranian woman had to renounce feminist ideas as 'petty bourgeois or bourgeois liberal deviations', and had to exclude the application of egalitarian ideals to private and sexual domains. As part of the opposition's counter-culture, the image of the 'authentic woman' (*zan-e asseel*) was constructed as practising selflessness or self-sacrifice, devotion to the family, and possessing virginity and chastity, humility, modesty, simplicity, excellent housekeeping, patience and endurance, and patriotism and loyalty to national and cultural values. This idealized image of the 'Eastern woman' was portrayed in contrast to that of the *farangi* woman, who was seen as selfish and individualistic.[38]

To understand the intellectual process that went into the cultural construction of these two contrasting images of women, I have examined the contemporary Iranian novel and social commentary of the post-Constitutional era, 1900-1970s.[39] In order to analyse changes in the conception of the 'Woman Question' in the mind of writers and social critics, I have reviewed the trend of change in the predominant images of women and gender-related issues in their writings. I discovered that the intellectuals' concern about women's oppression and their conceptualization of the 'Woman Question' took a progressive course up to the 1960s. But as we approach the 1978-79 Revolution, there seems to be a curious regressive trend in both the quantity and quality of writings on women's rights and women's images.

In the decade preceding the 1978-79 Revolution, the demand for women's rights and their public roles was no longer emphasized in the literary or political discourse of the opposition. The intellectuals were preoccupied with a painful search for a new identity. Attempts to counter 'cultural imperialism' and political repression, and concerns over economic exploitation by Western powers (mainly the US) had overshadowed their aspirations for modernization and socio-cultural progress. That is why, unlike the political discourse of the Constitutional Movement in which aspiration after modernity and progress was the dominant theme, in the 1978-79 movement, the issue of anti-imperialism and anti-monarchist dictatorship took on primary importance. While the most prominent and influential ideologues and social critics who paved the way for the Constitutional Movement were secular and modernist, those of the 1978-79 movement were oriented toward Islamic ideals.

The early reformers of Iran drew inspiration from the secular tendency of medieval Islamic philosophers like Ibn Rushd (Averroes); the nineteenth-century Babi movement in Iran;[40] and European philosophers of the Enlightenment like Rousseau and Locke. In the mid-nineteenth century, the early reformers opened up the debate over the 'Woman Question' for the first time in Iranian literature. They waged a many-sided campaign against internal reaction, religious repression, illiteracy and crippling traditions like the veil, polygyny, and seclusion of women. Mirza Aqa Khan Kirmani, an anti-religious nationalist glorifying pre-Islamic Iran, was probably the first to discuss the 'woman question' extensively in *Sad Khetabeh* (A Hundred Sermons) and in the newspaper he edited, *Akhtar*. Mirza Malkum Khan, a Paris-educated, anti-clerical Armenian-Iranian, made some references to women's issues in the columns of newspapers of this period, including *Qanoon*, which he began publishing in London in 1890. Jalil Mohammad Golizadeh (Molla Nasreddin), Fathali Akhundzadeh, and Talebof Tabrizi, all Azerbaijani-Iranian, wrote very influential social commentaries. One remarkable figure who was perhaps a source of inspiration for these early reformers is Zarintaj (Tahereh) Qurratul Ayn (1815-51). She joined the Babi movement and assumed a leading role in missionary activities. Her poetry, public preaching, intellectual debates with religious leaders, abandonment of her husband and relatives to join the movement, unveiling, fighting on the battlefield, and ultimately death as a martyr were unprecedented for a woman.[41] She qualified to serve as a significant indigenous role model for Iranian women. But her name and contributions have continued to be dismissed in Iranian mainstream literature, particularly because of her role in Babism.

The positive impact of the writings of these early modernist reformers on women later crystallized in women's participation in the Constitutional Movement, women's secret societies, their journalism, and in women activists such as Sadiqa Daulatabadi, Safia Yazdi, Badri Tundari, all of whom pioneered the women's movement in Iran.[42]

The expansion of girls' schools, education for women, and women's journalism left its mark on the literary and political discourse of the 1910-30 period. One predominant image that received much sympathy in the writings of the social critics and novelists of this period was the 'oppressed and victimized woman' whose condition resembled a 'slave', deprived of any human rights. She was seen as a victim of illiteracy, ignorance, superstition, and men's cruel and immoral abuse. This image was depicted in the writings of modernist intellectuals such as Dehkhoda, Jamalzadeh, Ishqi, and Lahuti who perceived women's emancipation as essential for modernization and the progress of Iranian society. They argued that the demand for women's education and public role was not just a Western idea, but rooted in Iranian native background. Referring to Iranian mythology and the national epic, they picked up positive, usually non-religious, female images of the pre-Islamic past as role models: Purandokht and Azarmidokht, two famous queens of the Sassanian period (AD 224-651); Gordafarid, a woman warrior who led the Iranians against a Turkish invasion;[43] Faranak, admired for her wisdom and intelligence; Katayoon, known for her determination and self-confidence; Homaay, a queen who ruled Iran for more than 30 years; Gordieyeh, praised for her leadership abilities, wisdom, and vision.[44] They were among the legendary women presented in the Shahnameh of Ferdowsi and other national epics dealing with the pre-Islamic history of Iran.

In the 1940s and 1950s the novels of writers such as Sadegh Hedayat, Abbas Khalili, Mahmood Hejazi, and Yahya Daulatabadi continued to depict women's oppression and victimization. They usually blamed men, the traditional culture, ignorance, and sometimes — cautiously and indirectly — the political structure as responsible for women's inferior and oppressed position. The main themes of this period included women's poverty; the sexual and emotional abuse of poor and naïve young girls by rich, corrupt and greedy men; and a gradually growing concern over the danger of promiscuity and moral degeneration of the youth.

But as modernization and Westernization expanded, and as the population of middle-class, urban, modernized women grew, a new image, namely of the *farangi* and 'bourgeois' woman, gradually appeared in the novels and social commentaries of the 1960s and 1970s. In the novels of writers such as Mohammad Massoud, Mohammad Ali Afghani, and Jalal Al-e Ahmad, the 'West-struck/Westoxicated' woman was depicted on the basis of those characteristics enumerated earlier in this chapter. This time, however, resentment, anger, and reproach replaced the earlier sympathy and support for women's public roles.[45] The Iranian intelligentsia, writers, poets, film-makers, and journalists, particularly those opposing the Shah's policies, expressed dismay at the Westernized, urban modern woman, while nostalgically admiring 'the authentic Iranian women'. In *Gharbzadegi*, Al-e Ahmad complained that a good woman could hardly be found in the big cities any more. Regretfully, he concluded that it was necessary to go to the countryside, to a village, to find a real Iranian woman. He claimed:

...woman who ought to be the preserver of the tradition, the family, the race and the lineage; has been brought on the streets. She has been led to wandering, showing herself off; behaving 'loose and unrestrained...[46]

Reza Baraheni, a prominent writer, professor, literary and social critic, in one of his major works, *The Masculine History: Dominant Culture and Dominated Culture*, similarly regrets the deteriorating trend in the character of the Iranian women:

As our old tales indicate, the Iranian woman in the past was, at least, a good housekeeper. She knew what kindness and purity meant. She was at least full of selflessness, ready to sacrifice herself for the sake of people around her. Today's urbanized woman is void of even these simple humane traits...[47]

Nowhere in his book, however, is urbanized man blamed for the loss of such 'simple humane traits'. Therefore, Baraheni, too, despite his valuable critique of the perspective of Iranian historians and despite his progressive stand on the 'Woman Question', maintained a rather masculine approach by employing double standards in his critique of Westernized men and women. In line with Ali Shariati and Al-e Ahmad, Baraheni's book addressed the problem of 'identity crisis' and contributed to the anti-Westoxication discourse of the 1960s and 1970s. Many Iranian intellectuals believed that the contemporary urban woman of Iran was in a more serious crisis of identity than was her male counterpart. Baraheni argued that the historical domination of men over women in Iran, and the absence of female role models in history, literature, arts, and textbooks even at the university level, had left the contemporary woman of Iran with no roots, no culture, no indigenous female role models. If she wanted to adopt an indigenous identity, she had to mimic Iranian male/masculine models. That is why she had no option other than to turn to foreign role models. The West-struck woman, therefore, is far more Westoxicated than is the West-struck man. She is far more identity-less, far more of a mimic, and far more alienated.[48]

Baraheni's secular, ostensibly Marxist, critiques, like those of Islamist intellectuals, denounced Westernized women. But rather than blaming the contemporary women for their loss of identity, he argued that they never had one to begin with. Such an approach, regardless of its merit, left the secular critics of 'Westoxication' in a disadvantaged position in comparison to the Islamists. For along with their rejection and denunciation of the contemporary Westernized image of womanhood, the Islamists, such as Shariati, also offered alternative role models, namely Fatimeh and Zeinab. Rather than treating women as mere victims of imperialism or historical patriarchy (as the leftists did), Islamists saw women as responsible and blamed them for having sinned against God by giving in to the imperialistic way of life, instead of following the path of their 'genuine' Islamic female models. The critique of most secular and leftist intellectuals was limited to negation, with almost no attempt to offer or affirm alternative role models for women. Neglecting the cultural dimension of the struggle, the left lacked an agenda for cultural deconstruction and reconstruction in different areas, including women's roles. The woman's image associated with the revolutionary left — a female guerrilla or an underground comrade — was one-dimensional, rather asexual, avant-garde, unreal, and irrelevant to the lay woman, thus far from an applicable role model.

In explaining the regressive trend in the intellectual discourse toward the 'Woman Question', the following historical background should also be noted. Since the nineteenth century, it had always been the reformist intellectuals and forces in opposition to the monarchy that had pushed for modernization and social change, including women's rights. But by the time the Shah's American-instigated reforms under the rubric of the 'White Revolution' started in 1961, it appeared that the Shah had taken over the banner of modernization and women's emancipation. But the progressive intelligentsia was unwilling to support the Shah's modernizing measures in the wake of increasing imperialistic influence and the Shah's dictatorship. They saw the Shah's 1953 coup against Mossadeq's government as actually reversing the genuine course of modernization and national development. Therefore, the progressive forces of opposition, not wanting to be seen to be complying with the Shah's modernization or his version of women's emancipation, kept a low profile on women's issues. While overlooking the reactionary nature of the clerics' opposition to the Shah's modernization, the intellectuals tried to focus their fight on the 'external forces of imperialism' and the Shah as the lackey or the 'internal base'. That is part of the reason why the left, and even Marxists, avoided ideological debates with the Islamic opposition over democratic issues like the 'Woman Question'.

Notwithstanding this criticism of the left, it should be noted that many leading activists and theoreticians of the contemporary Iranian feminist movement are actually former members or supporters of the Marxist organizations.

The political psychology of 'mostazaaf' and women

AS in their campaign against the Shah's Westernization, Islamic fundamentalists usually identified the masses as *mostazaafin* (the poor and powerless) and the rich and powerful as *mostakbarin*. Yet situating these terms within the political context of the time, they could not simply mean the poor versus the rich. For one reason, neither the pioneers of the fundamentalists, nor their primary constituency (bazaar merchants and traditional petty bourgeoisie) represented the real poor or the lower class. The two terms, more than an economic class distinction, did signify political and social-psychological dimensions of the fundamentalist discourse. It was actually not the reformists, but the more fundamentalist faction of the Islamic revivalists who introduced these unconventional terms into the political rhetoric of the anti-Shah movement. They deliberately tried to replace the then commonly used terminology of *oppression* and *exploitation* (known as part of the left and Marxist vocabulary) by the vague notion of *mostazaaf* which actually blurred the economic dimension of the conflict. In opposing the Shah's regime and Western influence in Iran, the left emphasized (or overemphasized) class analysis and economic disadvantages, for example, dependency, excessive exploitation of the masses, and the widening class disparity. The fundamentalists' main concern, however, seemed to be the Western cultural and ideological hegemony over the Iranian society. The issues of control, supremacy, political power, and boundary were central to the discourse of the clerics who led the fundamentalist uprising.

To retain their control over the hearts and minds of the people; to protect their boundaries of influence from shrinking in areas of education, law, and media; and to reverse the shifting boundary of women's role, the clergy had to address the question of political power and had to aim for its own political empowerment. The notion of *mostazaaf* actually projected the humiliated identity of the traditional segment of the middle class and most of all the clerics' own feeling of belittlement and weakening position in confrontation with modernization measures of the Westernized *mostakbarin* (the rich or the arrogant). The notion of *mostakbarin* was used in reference to snobbish and arrogant Western powers, the *Taghouti* (demonic) regime of the Shah, and whoever associated with them, including the rich and the emerging modernized women and men.

The *mostazaaf* was a frightened man. The imposed social transformation and the collapse of traditional values and ideals had led him to a state of incoherence. As Halpern cites: 'Incoherence can deepen to the point where death — by no longer caring enough or through a fanatic search for martyrdom — becomes preferable to further suffering.'[49] The passionate support for an Islamic alternative, fanatic adherence to the old ideals, and intense glorification of martyrdom are among the manifestations of a *mostazaaf* psyche.

A *mostazaaf*, whose control in the political, economic, and cultural construction of society has been diminishing, consciously or unconsciously holds on to the last boundary of his control, that is, women and children. The

family becomes his last hope and bastion of resistance. Halpern states that
people who live with incoherence become 'impotent, confused, apathetic, or
enraged as their bonds break'. They may try all the more to hold on to
connections — 'they become more loyal to family or ethnic group than ever
before...' Nikki Keddie and Lois Beck have made a similar point:

> The limits imposed on male freedom by religion and tradition and by the
> modern power of employers, government institutions, and Western incur-
> sions, may encourage men lacking wealth and power to keep control in the
> only area they can — that of women and children.[50]

The *mostazaaf* man tries to keep the family as an enclave protected from
the rest of the crisis milieu. In it, he wants to escape the pressures of the rapid
socio-economic changes and fierce competition. To compensate for his sense
of powerlessness and incapacity in the public sphere, he wants to ensure his
powerful status as patriarch in the household. He wants his obedient wife and
children to provide him with the emotional support necessary to boost his ego
and sense of pride, to revive him for the struggle against the *mostakbarin*. In a
mostazaaf's eyes, women's independence and strength leads to a crisis of
masculinity, a danger of emasculation, and a loss of *gheyrat*.[51] In his description of 'Westoxicated man', Al-e Ahmad addressed this very concern when he
criticized him for (among other things) being 'effeminate'.[52] Thus, for a man,
one precaution against Westoxication is to ensure that he was not seen as
'unmanly' or weak in his relations with women.

Therefore, the strong resistance against any changes in women's place
and the obsession over issues like the veil may actually represent a defence
mechanism for a man who suffers from insecurity and a shaky sense of
masculine identity. Of course, lack of separation of religion and state, and the
explicit patriarchal injunctions in the Quran (such as men's unilateral right to
divorce, polygyny, and the husband's consent as a requirement for a wife's
departure from the house) have come to the assistance of the *mostazaaf* man.
But it is not so much Islamic ideology as the question of power and control
which is responsible for the Muslim man's resistance to changes in women's
place and for his preoccupation with issues like *hijab*. As evidenced in post-
revolutionary Iran, whenever the ruling Islamists feel in control and their
political and economic conditions appear rather stable and strong (that is, less

mostazaaf), the pressure on women and issues like *hijab* ease considerably. This is why, whenever there is a renewed campaign in the Islamic republic against *bad-hijab* women (those who do not observe the Islamic dress code properly), women ask sarcastically: 'What is wrong with them again? Have they failed in another military action against Iraq? Have they suffered another economic or political set back? Or perhaps they have discovered another coup attempt!'

In short, Islamic *Sharia*, the deep, religiously embedded system of law, male-biased Islamic precepts, and traditional mechanisms like the veil, become conveniently meshed with political insecurity and psychological biases and fears forming an even stronger barrier against egalitarian changes in gender relations and family structure. This may explain why it has been the family, personal status, sexuality, and gender relations that Islamic law and custom have held onto most tenaciously. In contrast, certain Islamic civil and commercial codes, as well as regulations concerning eating and consuming conduct, have been modified or swept away with a bill or an Ayatollah's *fatva*.[53]

The 'Woman Question' after the revolution

SINCE the inception of the Islamic republic in 1979, the model of 'Islamic woman' has been officially promoted and forcefully imposed on Iranian women. But a quick overview of the present status of women in Iran and a study of the current Islamic discourse reveal that women's status and roles remain ambiguous. This is due in part to the fact that, among the ideologues and rulers of the Islamic republic, there is no unitary definition of Islamic society, no consensus on what constitutes truly Islamic womanhood, what constitutes proper *hijab*, and what constitutes an indigenous identity.

The ongoing contradictions in the policies of the Islamic regime and the present multiplicity in women's roles and images in the Islamic discourse demonstrate that the ideology of Islam, particularly when it takes over the state machinery in the twentieth century, must come to some accommodation with the modern world.[54] The militant Islamic fundamentalists, having assumed state power, are no longer *mostazaaf*. Their material and psychological conditions have experienced profound changes. For example: In 1988, Ayatollah Montazeri (who was originally designated to succeed Khomeini), in one of his lectures on women's role in Islamic society, referred to *Nahjolbalageh*, an

important Islamic text by the first Imam, Ali, for whom Shia Muslims hold the
highest regard. He specifically cited one of Ali's testaments commanding his
son Hassan (the second Imam) that:

> Avoid taking any counsel from women because their opinions are faulty and
> their decisions inconstant. Cover them with *hijab* because *hijab* would keep
> them safer and purer. Their going out of the house is as bad as letting
> strangers and unreliable persons go among them. If you can prevent her from
> getting to know anybody, do that.[55]

The tenets of this command are in obvious contradiction, not only with the
social roles, behavioural patterns, and unveiled appearance of a modernized
secular woman, but also with the active participation of Islamic veiled women
in politics and social affairs, both during and after the Revolution of 1979.

The president of the Islamic republic, Hojatoleslam Hashemi Rafsanjani,
in a meeting with a group of female participants in a shooting contest and
religious scholarship (5 July 1990) emphasized that:

> In the Islamic society all the means are provided for ladies to become active
> in public life. Our ladies' way of social activism should be introduced to the
> world as a model ... All those dedicated and faithful women of our country
> who participate in the public life are pioneers of women's Islamic move-
> ment ... A female student of religion (*talabeh*) can become a high school
> teacher, elementary school teacher, researcher, writer and jurisconsult
> (*faqih*). She only needs to observe the Islamic mores... Ladies can become
> philosophers, preachers, and even Imams (of Friday Prayers). This is not
> only compatible with chastity, but can actually promote it.[56]

In the same meeting Rafsanjani criticized those fanatics who view the female
voice as profane and said that 'we witnessed how Imam Khomeini himself
listened to women's talks on radio and television and promoted them'.[57]

In one of his political and religious decrees in 1963, Khomeini, as a then
less-known member of the opposition to the Shah, specifically protested against
women's suffrage that the Shah had declared in the same year. But after taking
power, the same Khomeini made special effort to mobilize women to vote for
his Islamic republic and subsequent measures. At the same time, the Family

Protection Acts of 1967 and 1975, which curbed some of men's unilateral rights, were abrogated by the Islamist government. Apart from mandatory *hijab*, Khomeini's government lowered the age of consent for girls from eighteen to thirteen (under nine in some circumstances), reinstated polygamy, temporary marriage, and unilateral divorce by men and custody of their children, severely restricted sexuality and reproductive rights, established sex-segregation of public areas, workplaces, school, and universities, banned certain fields of higher education for women (such as law, agriculture, geology, archaeology), and launched a public campaign to tie women to maternal roles.

During the last few years, however, there have been some changes in the position of women. Owing to insufficient empirical and independent research reports from Iran, it is very difficult to assess the real impact on women's situation of these past ten years of the Islamic government's rule. The following general observations draw from secondary sources and my own content analysis of women's journals and publications in Iran, as well as personal contacts with Iranian activists and women's groups inside and outside Iran.

Despite the regressive policies and discriminatory attitudes of the Islamic government toward women, the present situation for women does not appear as gloomy as it did immediately after the Revolution. Certain recent trends in women's activities in Iran are encouraging and hopeful. With respect to women's work, and using data for 1983-84, Moghadam showed that much of the initial rhetoric of the Islamic republic attempting to impose an ideology of domesticity has not been successful. She noted for example that:

> Although labour participation rates have declined for women, they have declined even more for men. The female share of the urban labour force (11.2 per cent) has not altered, and government employment for women is actually higher today than it was before the Revolution.[58]

Moghadam offered a number of factors to explain this: a discrepancy between pre-industrial ideological prescriptions and economic imperatives of capitalist development in Iran; the exigencies of the eight-year war with Iraq; economic need on the part of some women and resistance to total subjection on the part of others (especially educated women with previous work experience); and the ambiguities in the discourse and policies of the Islamic political élite and the conflicting cultural images of women. These factors, she argued, allowed women to participate in the formal economy and to manoeuvre within the confines of the Islamic system. Another factor I believe should be added is the enormous brain drain (mostly male), which leaves the regime short of skilled 'manpower', thus creating a need for the available women professionals.

In a comparative study of pre- and post-revolutionary statistics regarding female literacy in Iran, Mehran dismisses the widely held belief that the Islamic republic shuns any form of education for girls.[59] But, as she demonstrates, the decrease in the female illiteracy rate since the Revolution has been very small (from 63.5 per cent in 1975 to 61 per cent in 1985). Iranian women's literacy rate has fallen behind many of their Middle Eastern and North African counterparts. Female education at the second level, especially in rural areas, has suffered some setback mainly because of sex segregation. Women's education at the university level, however, has not experienced a drastic setback as far as attainment and enrolment levels are concerned. In 1975, female student enrolment was 28 per cent and female instructors 14 per cent — in 1985 they increased to 30 per cent and 16 per cent respectively. But, as Mehran notes, 'there has been a deliberate policy to redirect educational and occupational choices among women' toward traditional women's fields.[60] However, since 1988, several attempts have been made to revise and modify the sex discriminatory restrictions against women's higher education. In her analysis, Mojab attributes this latest reformist trend to women students' resistance and the push for educational equity.[61]

Several female artists, poets, and writers have become prominent in post-revolutionary Iran. Their works are occasionally woman-oriented and reflective of feminist consciousness. For instance, Shahrnoosh Parsipur is a young feminist writer and a former political prisoner whose works have become best-sellers. She is the first woman writer in Iranian history to receive offers of publication contracts before completion of her work.[62] Incidentally, since the publication of her latest collection of short stories — *Women Without Men* (1989) — she has been under attack by the fundamentalists and briefly arrested again (for a short while this time) for her courageously sarcastic critique of 'the cult of virginity' and double standards over sex.[63]

Despite the ideological censorship and crippling rules imposed on film-makers against women's appearance in cinema, there have been encouraging signs in recent Iranian movies. While in pre-revolutionary Iran women's images in movies were usually negative, one-dimensional, and limited to the traditional mother, passive lover or temptress, in several recent and most popular films, some positive, strong, and active images have been portrayed of women with their own independent indigenous identities and multi-dimensional social roles.[64]

In addition to the factors enumerated above, which have shaped women's status in post-revolutionary Iran, one further factor that needs to be elaborated here is the development of a reformist approach that I tentatively call 'Islamist feminism'. This is a growing activism among Islamist women élite who are pushing for a reform within an Islamic framework.

In the attempt by the fundamentalists to regain Islamic identity and to reaffirm the model of Islamic womanhood, those women who decisively adhered to that model and participated in the Revolution became the symbol of the transformation of society, thus gaining status as bearers and maintainers of cultural heritage and religious values.[65] Khomeini frequently praised those women by calling them 'the real teachers of men in the noble movement of Islam' or 'the symbol of the actualization of Islamic ideals'. In their attempt to monopolize state power and to counter the forces of their rival revolutionaries — the left and reformist Islamists like the *Mojahedin* — the clerics had to keep their women supporters politically active in the years after the Revolution. Participation in politics and in the social sphere both during and after the Revolution has been a turning point in the lives of those women who mostly had a traditional middle-class background. Of course, the official mobilization of women was intended to strengthen the Islamic state, not liberate women. Nevertheless, the very politicization of women and their continuous exposure to ideological and political challenges of the opposition forces, particularly the growing secular feminism among Iranian women, has made it increasingly difficult for the Islamic state to redomesticate and privatize them.

These strata of women, who have now (unlike under the Shah) gained status and a legitimate, respected identity, feel empowered and self-confident. Paradoxically, these women seem to have appropriated some of the political purposes of the veil to their own advantage. That is, the revival of piety and the Islamic dress code are being utilized by these women as a means of gaining access to the public sphere. They argue that, in an Islamic society regulated and sanctified by the clerics and immunized against Westoxication by *hijab*, women's public role should no longer be a source of *fitna* or moral disorder.

The impact of the ideological challenges and an international political campaign by the opposition against women's place in the orthodox doctrine of Islam and the Islamic government's sexist policies on the one hand, and these Islamist women's own social praxis and daily confrontation with the patriarchal barriers on the other hand, seem to have further influenced their perception of gender roles, thus leading them to a reformistic approach toward Islam, an approach more in line with Shariati than the conservative clerics.[66] These women demand to see Islam practised in its 'true spirit' in which they believe that oppressed women can find salvation. They have started their own study groups, associations and publications, as well as their own exegesis and interpretation of the Quran, gradually generating a new woman-oriented reformist discourse in Islam.

For instance, Maryam Gorji, a former woman representative in the Islamic Parliament, who was known to be indifferent to, and ignorant of, women's issues, is now engaged in writing a woman-centred reinterpretation of women's images in the Quran.[67] Khomeini's daughter, Zahra Mostafavi, founded the 'Association of Muslim Women' in 1989, and, copying Western women, she has organized international women's conferences in Tehran. The women's university Al-Zahra has initiated the establishment of a Centre for the Study of Women. A state-affiliated Women's Council and several women's commissions have been established recently to study and help out women with their specific concerns.

Although during the 1980s women's representation in the Islamic Parliament (*Majlis*) was limited to four women out of 286 (nine women were elected in 1992), some of them were quite vocal in raising women's issues and in criticizing the government's policies. They have been successful in their intervention in areas such as the family and education. The leading figures among these Islamist women élite have usually been associated with men in power (Zahra Rahnavard, the wife of the former Prime Minister Musavi; Azam Taleqani, the daughter of the late, prominent Ayatollah Taleqani; and Ateqeh Sadiqi, the wife of the slain Prime Minister Radjaei). These women have been influential in the recent reforms in marriage and family law which provide some restrictions against men's unilateral rights to divorce, child custody, and polygamy similar to those of the Pahlavi state's Family Protection Act.

The ideological contradictions and conflicts with Quranic injunctions that these reform-minded women have to grapple with are predictable. But their potential for success among many young and old women, the new challenges that they bring into the feminist discourse, and their prospective impact on the 'Woman Question' in Iran have yet to be explored and theorized. Some Iranian socialist-feminists have already suggested exploring possibilities for dialogue, and strategies of issue-oriented co-ordination of actions, between Islamic and secular feminists.[68] But the undemocratic, sectarian, and exclusive nature of the 'Islamist feminists' has prevented any such *rapprochement*. Their version of feminism, if any, is based on an essentialistic approach emphasizing sex differences. Philosophically, it appears that a form of 'cultural feminism' represents, to some extent, a Western counterpart of these Islamic women's ideas and practices. Some scholars have endorsed Islamist 'veiled activism' in countries like Egypt as feminist, 'dignifying', and 'humanizing' to women.[69] But one should distinguish between women in the opposition who choose 'veiled activism' as a mechanism to participate in social and political life, and those Islamists in power who impose the veil on women to impart a uniformed Islamic identity and utilize a controlled female activism as a political advantage for the consolidation of the state power.

Summary and conclusion

THIS chapter has examined the place of women in the political and ideological discourses of pre- and post-revolutionary Iran. It has shown how the 'Woman Question' became part of an ideological terrain upon which concerns about national identity, development and modernization, cultural and moral integrity were articulated and debated by the Iranian intelligentsia, particularly the Islamists. By placing these events in retrospect, this chapter has analysed the process that went into the production of the Islamic model of womanhood. The Islamic model that emerged as a counter-culture at odds with the modernization paradigm of the Shah's regime, initially served as a defence mechanism and a response to the psychological quest for a personal as well as social identity on the part of the younger generation of the traditional middle-class women. It eventually became one of the central components of the political culture and ideological discourse of the Islamic Republic of Iran.

I have further argued that 'the model of Islamic woman' in Iran has taken on new characteristics which are distinct from, and in some respects contradictory to, the image of a domesticated woman promoted by the Islamic clerics in the initial stages of the Revolution. Among (élite and non-élite) Muslim women active in the socio-political arena, a new consciousness or a reformist trend, which some have called 'Islamist feminism', is quietly evolving. This trend opens up new prospects for Iranian women in general and new challenges for secular feminists in particular. It may change the dimensions, conception, and definition of women's identity and the woman question for the younger generation of Iranian women and men.

In common with women in many other Muslim countries, the most difficult challenge for Iranian feminists is to maintain a delicate balance between reclaiming a national identity, reaffirming progressive elements of the indigenous culture, and the struggle to create a democratic, just, and coherently developed society. This would be a society that moves beyond both neo-colonial subordination and regressive traditions by subscribing to women's liberation and gender equity.

Notes

1. K Sacks, *Sisters and Wives: The Past and Future of Sexual Inequality* (Westport, Conn: Greenwood, 1979), p. 101.

2. B Jazani, *Capitalism and Revolution in Iran* (London: Zed Press, 1980).

3. The issue of women's suffrage was raised once during the *Majlis* debates with vehement opposition from the clergy. See Eliz Sanasarian, *The Women's Rights Movement in Iran: Mutiny, Appeasement and Repression from 1900 to Kho*meini (New York: Praeger, 1982).

4. H Alavi, 'The State in Post-Colonial Societies', *New Left Review* 74 (1972).

5. P Worsley, *The Three Worlds: Culture and Development* (Chicago: University of Chicago Press, 1984).

6. M Halpern, 'Four Contrasting Repertories of Human Relations in Islam', in C Brown and N Itzkowitz (eds.) *Psychological Dimensions of Near Eastern Studies* (Princeton: The Darwin Press, 1977), p. 97.

7. Ibid., pp. 96-7.

8. W Ogburn, *On Culture and Social Change* (University of Chicago Press, 1964).

9. See FH Cardoso, 'Dependency and Development in Latin America', in Hamza Alavi and Teodor Shanin (eds.) *Introduction to the Sociology of Developing Societies* (New York: Monthly Review Press, 1982), pp. 112-27.

10. J Bill and C Leiden, *Politics in the Middle East* (New York: Little Brown & Company, 1984), pp. 2-3.

11. See V Moghadam, 'The Critical and Sociological Approach in Middle East Studies', *Critical Sociology* 17 (1) (1990), pp. 111-24.

12. R Hammami and M Rieker, 'Feminist Orientalism and Oriental Marxism', *New Left Review* 171 (1988), p. 101.

13. E Boserup, *Women's Role in Economic Development* (New York: St. Martin's Press, 1970); B Rogers, *The Domestication of Women: Discrimination in Developing Societies* (New York: St. Martin's Press, 1980); L. Beneria, *Women and Development: The Sexual Division of Labour in Rural Societies* (New York: Praeger, for the International Labour Office, 1982); G Sen and C Grown, *Development, Crisis, and Alternative Visions: Third World Women's Perspectives* (New York: Monthly Review Press, 1987); Sacks, op. cit.; H Papanek, 'Implications of Development for Women in Indonesia: Selected Research and Policy Issues', Center for Asian Development Studies, Discussion Paper No. 8, Boston University, Mass (1979); I Tinker (ed.) *Persistent Inequalities: Women and World Development* (New York: Oxford University Press, 1990).

14. E Friedl, 'Women and the Division of Labor in an Iranian Village' (Merip Reports, 95, 1981), p. 18. See also A Tabari, 'Islam and the Struggle for Emancipation of Iranian Women', in A Tabari and N Yeganeh (eds.) *In the Shadow of Islam: The Women's Movement in Iran* (London: Zed Press, 1982); S Shahshahani, *Char Fasl-e aftab: zendegi-e ruzmarreh-e zanan-e oscan yafteh ashayer Mamsani* (Four-Seasons of Sun: Women's Daily Lives Among the Settled Mamasani Tribues) (Tehran: Toos Publishers, 1987).

15. Friedl, op. cit., p. 18.

16. See, for example, A Aghajanian, 'The Impact of Development on the Status of Women: A District Level Analysis in Iran', *Journal of Developing Societies* 8 (1991), pp. 292-8; E Sanasarian, 'The Politics of Gender and Development in the Islamic Republic of Iran', *Journal of Developing Societies* 8 (1991), pp. 56-68; V Moghadam, 'Development and Women's Emancipation: Is There A Connection?', *Development and Change* 23 (3)(July 1992), pp. 215-56.

17. See H Saffioti, *Women in Class Society* (New York: Monthly Review Press, 1978); J Nash and I S Safa (eds.) *Sex and Class in Latin America* (New York: Praeger, 1976).

18. Tabari, op. cit., p. 27.

19. H Nayer, 'Sahm-e Zanan dar Rustay-e Negari' (Women's Contribution in Negari Village); *Mofid*, a monthly report published in Tehran Vol. 3, No. 4 (July 8-11, 1987); B Shahmoradi, 'Zanan-e Bakhtiari' (Women of Bakhtiar), *Mofid*: 8 (Tehran, pp. 40-44, 1987); Shahshahani, op. cit.

20. Tabari, op. cit., p. 7.

21. Janet Bauer, cited in M E Hegland, 'Traditional Iranian Women: How They Cope', *The Middle East Journal* 30 (4) (1982), pp. 483-501.

22. A Betteridge, 'The Controversial Vows of Urban Muslim Women in Iran', in N Falk and R Gross (eds), *Unspoken Worlds: Women's Religious Lives in Non-Western Cultures* (San Francisco: Harper and Row, 1980), pp. 141-55.

23. Estimate is based on 'Statistics of the Ministry of Higher Education of Iran: Center for Educational Planning' (in Persian) (Tehran 1984). See also G Mehran, 'The Education of a New Muslim Woman in Postrevolutionary Iran', paper presented at the VIIth World Congress of Comparative Education, Montreal, Canada (1989).

24. Tabari, op. cit., p. 8.

25. F Mernissi, *Beyond the Veil, Male-Female Dynamics in Modern Muslim Society* (revised edition) (Bloomington: Indiana University Press, 1987).

26. N Tohidi, 'Gender and Islamic Fundamentalism: Feminist Politics in Iran', in C T Mohanty, A Russo and L Torres, *Third World Women and the Politics of Feminism* (Bloomington: Indiana University Press, 1991).

27. While using certain images of Islamic legends, Shariati played a key role in the reconstruction of the female role models for the new Islamic movement. The image of Fatimeh (the daughter of the Prophet Mohammad and the wife of Ali, the First Imam) represented essential traits and dimensions of the ideal character of Islamic woman, such as loyalty and devotion to family, immense tolerance, compassion, feminine modesty, and chastity (*hojb, haya*). Zeinab (daughter of Fatimeh and the sister of Hossein, the Third Imam and the Hero of Karbala tragedy), on the other hand, represented a heroine image — a useful role model for mobilizing Muslim women during the revolution. Zeinab's political militancy, immense courage, great gift of oratory, and incredible defiance in the face of oppressive forces were emphasized to symbolize the necessary characteristics of a new revolutionary Muslim woman.

28. See N Yeganeh, 'Women's Struggles in the Islamic Republic of Iran', in A Tabari and N Yeganeh (eds.) op. cit.

29. D Baxter, 'A Palestinian Women's Islamic Group on the West Bank', paper presented at the annual meeting of the Middle East Studies Association, Toronto (1989).

30. E H Erikson, *Identity: Youth and Crisis* (New York: W W Norton, 1966).

31. The Iranian *Mojahedin*, along with Shariati, represented the non-clerical trends of reform and revision within the Islamist movement. The *Mojahedin* actually recruited many of their members (men and women) from among the students and followers of Shariati. Compared to Shariati, however, the *Mojahedin* represented a radical and eclectic version of Islam, borrowing certain elements from Marxism. In their strategy that followed armed urban guerrilla tactics. See E Abrahamian, *Radical Islam: The Iranian Mojahedin* (London: I B Tauris, 1989).

32. P Higgins, 'Women in the Islamic Republic of Iran: Legal, Social, and Ideological Changes', pp. 477-94 in *Signs*, Vol. 10, No. 3 (1985), p. 490.

33. N Kabeer, 'Subordination and Struggle: Women in Bangladesh', *New Left Review* 168 (1988), pp. 95-121.

34. Fatemi N Sayfpur, 'Nehzat-e azadi-ye zan dar Iran' (Women's Freedom Movement in Iran), *Rahavard* (a Persian Journal of Iranian Studies) (Los Angeles, 20/21, 1988),

pp. 76-92; E. Sanasarian, op. cit.

35. See Bill and Leiden, op. cit., for a discussion of patrimonialism. For a discussion of the nation as family, see H J Wiarda, *Political and Social Change in Latin America* (Boston: University of Massachusetts Press, 1974), p. 275.

36. A Jagger, *Feminist Politics and Human Nature* (New Jersey: Rowman & Allanheld, 1983).

37. A Rassam, 'Arab Women: The Status of Research in the Social Sciences and the Status of Women', in *Social Science Research and Women in the Arab World,* Frances Pinter Publishers for UNESCO, Paris (1984), p. 12.

38. Many religious and secular political intellectuals came to believe that consumerism, hedonism, preoccupation with sexual and sensual pleasures were manifestations of 'cultural imperialism', political apathy, and moral degeneration. As a defensive reaction to this, a sort of somatophobia (fear of body) and 'pleasure anxiety' became prevalent among the pre-revolutionary activists. These terms are from W Reich, *The Function of the Orgasm* (New York: Simon and Schuster, 1973). Puritanical attitudes, obsession with women's bodies, attempts to asexualize the revolutionaries, neglect of sexual desires and physical appearance, and dismissal of leisure activities gave activists a stern, grim, and stoic image. Besides ideological and attitudinal reasons behind such behavioural patterns, they were required, in part, to prepare the activists for probable imprisonment and torture under the omnipresent danger of SAVAK, the secret police.

39. In this particular investigation, I was inspired by D Kandiyoti, 'Slave Girls, Temptresses, and Comrades: Images of Women in the Turkish Novel', *Feminist Issues,* (Spring 1988).

40. Babism, later known as Baha'ism, was a heretical movement founded in Iran in the 1840s. It advocated social reforms, demanded freedom of trade and rights of personal property, the reduction of unjust taxes, a higher status for women, limits on polygamy, a prohibition on violence against women, and measures for their education, see N Keddie, *Roots of Revolution: An Interpretive History of Modern Iran* (New Haven, Conn: Yale University Press, 1981), p. 50.

41. See M Bayat-Phillips, 'Women and Revolution in Iran 1905-11', in L Beck and N Keddie (eds.) *Women in the Muslim World* (Cambridge, Mass: Harvard University Press, 1982), pp. 295-307.

42. Sanasarian, op. cit.

43. K Jayawardena, *Feminism and Nationalism in the Third World* (London: Zed Books, 1986).

44. P Shakeeba, 'Naqsh va tasveer-e zan dar Shahnameh-ye Ferdowsi' (The Role and Image of Woman in Shahnameh of Ferdowsi), *Nimeye-digar* , (Persian Language Feminist Journal), Nos. 6 and 7 (1988), pp. 28-62, 32-62.

45. N Tohidi, 'Masale-ye zan va rowshanfekran dar daheha-ye akhir' (The Woman

Question and Intellectuals over the past Decades), *Nimeye-digar* 10 (1990), pp. 51-95.

46. J Al-e Ahmad, *Gharzadegi* (Tehran, 1964), p. 51, emphasis added.

47. R Baraheni, *Tarikhe mozakkar: farhange hakem, farhange mahkoom* (The Masculine History: Dominant Culture and Dominated Culture) (Tehran, 1972), p. 29.

48. Ibid., pp. 29-32.

49. Halpern, op. cit., p. 96.

50. N Keddie and L Beck, 'Introduction', pp. 1-34 in L Beck and N Keddie (eds.)*Women in the Muslim World* (Cambridge, Mass: Harward University Press, 1982), p. 28.

51. The term *gheyrat* is rich in connotation and is usually used in a masculine context referring to men's zeal, sense of pride, honour, and jealousy toward their women.

52. Al-e J Ahmad, op. cit., p. 147.

53. For example, usury and any practice of lending money with an interest charge (*rebh*) is prohibited in Islam. Thus, by principle, there should be an ideological barrier against banking and financial capitalism in an Islamic government. In practice, however, by a virtual stroke of the pen of the ayatollahs, the interest charged by the Iranian banks has been pronounced as legitimate commission or service fee.

54. Bill and Leiden, op. cit., p. 68.

55. *Nahjolbalagheh*, Letter 31, Feyz/938 LH/405.

56. *Zan-e Ruz* (Today's Woman) 1272, (Tehran, 1990), p. 5.

57. Ibid.

58. See V Moghadam, 'Women, Work, and Ideology in the Islamic Republic', pp. 221-43 in *International Journal of Middle Eastern Studies*, Vol. 20 (1988), p. 221.

59. Mehran, op. cit.

60. Ibid, p. 17.

61. S Mojab, 'State Control and Women's Resistance in the Universities of Iran', paper presented at the First Conference of Iranian Women's Studies Foundation, Cambridge, Mass (Harvard University, 1990).

62. F Milani, *Veils and Words: The Emerging Voices of Iranian Women Writers* (New York: Syracuse University Press, 1992).

63. Two other novels by Parsipur that received rave reviews are *Tuba va maanaye shab* (Tuba and the Meaning of the Night), (Tehran, 1989); and *sag va zemestan-e bowland* (The Dog and the Long Winter) (Tehran, 1976).

64. For instance, see the films *Tenants* and *Hamoun* directed by Mehrjuei, reviewed by the *New York Times*, 15 August 1990, and particularly the film *Bashu: the Little Stranger* by Beizaei, reviewed in *Los Angeles Times* and *LA Weekly*, 8 June 1990.

65. YY Haddad and E B Findly (eds.) *Women, Religion and Social Change* (Albany: State University of New York Press, 1985), p. 275.

66. In spring 1990, for the first time in post-revolutionary Iran, a three-day seminar was held in commemoration of Ali Shariati at the University of Tehran. One of the speakers

who presented a strongly supportive lecture was Zahra Rahnavard. This provides yet another sign of the growing trend toward a reformist modern version of Islam among the more educated supporters of the Islamic Republic.

67. Several parts of Gorji's interpretation (*tafsir*) of 'Women in Quran' appeared in *Zan-e Ruz* (Tehran, March to May issues, 1990).

68. Yeganeh, op. cit., and Moghadam, op. cit. (1988).

69. F El Guindi, 'Veiled Activism: Egyptian Women in the Contemporary Islamic Movement', *Femmes de la Méditerranée Peuples/Méditerranéens* 22-23 (January-June 1983).

Chapter 7

Nationalism and Feminism: Palestinian women and the *Intifada* — No Going Back?

Nahla Abdo

'NO GOING Back' is a statement quite often reiterated by women activists in the ongoing Palestinian *Intifada*. With an indirect reference to the Algerian experience and a direct one to their own history of subjugation, Palestinian women appear to be making a historical breakthrough. What is the material basis for this strong conviction about difference and change? Is it the heat of the *Intifada,* which appears to be temporarily dispersing some of the age-old differences within Palestinian traditional society? Or is there a genuine process of social, economic and cultural change in which women are engaged and vow to nourish, even after national independence?

Intifada in Arabic can be translated as a spontaneous awakening that results from a hard strike or a shock (the origin of the word is *Intafad*, that is, to wake up with a jolt); and it denotes a process of a fundamental shake-up or house-cleaning (the origin here is *nafad* or everything turned upside-down). As far as the *Intifada* is concerned, it is fruitless to search for any spontaneous, unplanned, or unorganized movement. The *Intifada* involves a process of fundamental change. What needs to be investigated is the character of this movement and the nature of women's participation. Questions to be addressed here include: what has changed in Palestinian social-gender relations? how fundamental is this change to both Palestinian society at large and women in particular? how is nationalism — as an ideology which masks gender and class — perceived by women activists? In other words, what are the new social, political, economic, and cultural foundations for women's belief in real or potential fundamental change?

To answer these questions, the relationship between feminism and nationalism will be examined by placing the Palestinian women's struggle within a historical framework. Research for this chapter is based on fieldwork in the West Bank and Gaza Strip during summer 1990. Most of the interviews took place in Beit Sahour (the West Bank) and Beit Hanoun (Gaza Strip) in June and July 1990. And as part of my study of the economic dimension of the *Intifada*, I also visited several co-operative projects on the West Bank.

Some theoretical considerations

A MAJOR conceptual problem here concerns the relationship between women's emancipation and national liberation. Nationalism is not a neutral form of expression. Despite the historical character it acquires as an anti-colonial form of struggle, nationalism is not about gender, 'class', religious, or ethnic freedoms. When, in 1983, Benedict Anderson wrote that: '[N]ationalism has proved an uncomfortable anomaly for Marxist theory and precisely for that reason, has been largely elided, rather than confronted',[1] national struggles were still largely confined to Third World countries. Then, one could comfortably identify two major national struggles; the South African and the Palestinian. Today, it is clear that the 1990s have ushered in a new historical phase in the development of the national question. Stormy debates within the Canadian government over the Meech Lake Accords, and the question of Quebec as a 'Distinct Society', acted as a constant reminder while writing this chapter. National sovereignty has ceased to be a burning issue for Third World peoples only. Even the specifically anti-colonial and anti-imperialist nature of nationalism does not seem to be the primary concern for national struggles.

Recent dramatic events in Eastern Europe, together with the separatist nationalist movements in the former Soviet Union, have left very few doubts about the multiplicity of forms and aims of nationalism. The task of defining, and more so redefining, nationalism in the face of all these complexities, requires extensive and collective efforts. Any comprehensive definition of the issue is likely to be contingent on the future outcome of these new national/ist movements.

None the less, for the purpose of this study, nationalism will be used in a very specific context — namely, as far as it intersects with women's mobilization in the national struggle. From past historical experience, it is clear that women have been largely excluded from taking an active leadership role in national struggles. In cases where women did participate actively, their experiences appear to be quite bitter. In almost all liberation movements where women were actively involved, a general reversal of their roles became the fact of life after national liberation and the establishment of the nation-state.

The nation-state and gender policies

THE literature suggests that the ideology of nationalism is a strong force capable of using, misusing and abusing its female participants. Nationalism in general promotes a specific discourse on women. In this discourse, women are identified as maintainers and reproducers of 'national soldiers, national heroes and manpower'. Nationalism can also be used as a double-edged weapon: as a mechanism of domination and oppression and as a potential force for gender-social liberation.

While this chapter is concerned with the second form of nationalism — the struggle for liberation — some characteristic features of women's mobilization in maintaining and reproducing state-institutionalized nationalism will be discussed briefly. Official nationalism constructs an ideology of motherhood which relegates women to the home by focusing on women's appropriate arena for fostering national identity through their child-rearing and domestic responsibilities as wives and mothers.[2] Biological and social reproduction is seen as women's divinely-ordained responsibility.

Irrespective of its form, a nation-state that conceives of women's role primarily as reproducers carries with it the seeds not only of sexist discrimination but also of ethnic/racial discrimination. This is true in the case of Israel where the need for an exclusive Jewish state and Jewish mothers has been an inherent feature of Israel's political and juridical institutions. Thus, Israeli-Jewish women were expected to reproduce the Jewish nation at home as well as international Jewry abroad. Jewish mothers need 'to have enough children to "compensate" for the children lost in the Nazi Holocaust and to what is called in Israel the "demographic Holocaust" and assimilation'.[3]

While the means vary for implementing gender policies by nation-states, the nature of these policies is often oppressive. Within the Israeli context, Jewish nationalism, which is used as a euphemism for what is, in reality, demographic racism, produces racially divided gender policies. In addition to its use of economic and political means (such as limiting access to education, work and social mobility) to discourage the Palestinian Arab population, Israel adopts racially-biased gender policies towards its own female citizens. These include lowering national insurance benefits for Arab children and encouraging abortion clinics and free contraceptives for Arab women. At the same time, Israel has done everything possible to encourage the birthrate by placing obstacles to Jewish women's access to contraceptives and providing other incentives, such as 'The Fund for Encouraging Birth', which was established to 'subsidize housing loans for Jewish families with more than three children'.[4]

Constructing women's identity on an exclusively racial or ethnic basis is equally true of the South African regime. The enfranchisement of women in a Bill introduced in 1930 read: '*Woman* means a woman who is wholly of European parentage, extraction or descent.' From the point of view of the Apartheid regime, 'mothers have a crucial role in personally supporting and validating military solutions in the opposition to Apartheid'.[5] Such policies are not exclusive to undemocratic states. Liberal democracies such as Britain and the United States are well-known for subjugating poor women and women of colour into forced sterilization or the use of the infamous Depo-Provera cancerous birth-control devices.[6]

These examples show that it is necessary to distinguish, theoretically and politically, between an oppressive state national ideology and the ideology of a national liberation struggle. None the less, it is imperative for the women and men engaged in national struggle to realize the potentially oppressive feature of institutionalized nationalism. For example, elements of the Palestinian national culture were formed in response to the Israeli political culture. Historically, Palestinian nationalism has capitalized on notions such as 'the mother of the martyr' or 'the fertile mother-nation' on the one hand, and 'Palestine as the Fathers' land', on the other. Slogans like 'Israelis beat us at the borders but we beat them in the bedrooms', or Mahmoud Darwish's well-known poem, 'Write down I am an Arab ... I have eight children and the ninth will come next summer ... Are you angry?' manifest the deep national culture of Diaspora Palestinians. As national-popular values that partly define Palestinian identity and integrity, these cultural artifacts are, none the less, sexist and objectionable to women.

Unlike institutionalized forms of nationalism, however, national culture produced in the course of struggle has the potential to be emancipatory and progressive. But this depends on the extent of women's active involvement as well as their success in pushing women's issues to the forefront of the national agenda. The emancipatory aspect of the national liberation movement is equally dependent on the degree to which it is capable of articulating its struggle with the class struggle. Below I assess the Palestinian national struggle in terms of its gender and class components.

Gender, class, and the Palestinian national struggle

IT IS important to reconstruct one dimension of the Palestinian history which has received scant attention, that is women's participation in the national struggle prior to the *Intifada*. Three historical phases of women's development will be identified: (1) 1920-48; (2) 1949-67; and (3) the period since 1967. This periodization is not as simple as it may appear, for the continuum includes discontinuities. Except for the first phase, 1920-48, evolution of Palestinian culture in general, and particularly in respect to women, has been dramatically disrupted. The material conditions and consequent ideological and cultural modes of relations that developed among Palestinians after 1948 vary radically from one community to the other. Palestinians who remained in Palestine after the creation of the state of Israel, and who were placed under military rule and turned into second-class minority citizens, were involved in specific forms of struggle and survival. Different forms of survival and struggle were pursued by the majority of Palestinians expelled from Palestine after 1948. Moreover, depending on the political-economic order of each 'host' country, social and gender relations among Palestinians varied from one region to another.

Phase One: 1920-48

DURING this period Palestinians were faced with two forms of oppressive rule: British colonialism and Zionist settlerism. These forces intensified the process of Palestinian transformation, gradually eroding the relatively self-sufficient traditional agrarian economy. The expropriation of more than 23 per cent of Palestine's cultivated land and the consequent proletarianization of the peasants has affected one of the major social/cultural structures of the Palestinian society, namely, the Palestinian *hamula* or extended family.

The traditional *hamula* was not an undifferentiated unit of mutual interdependency. It was hierarchical, patriarchal, and based on gender, age and class differences. This is particularly true since the development of capitalism in Palestine at the turn of the twentieth century.[7] The *hamula* structure was more prevalent among landlords and rich peasants than among poor peasants and the landless. None the less, *hamula*-based cultural values remained hegemonic. Through endogamous marriage and traditional exclusion from property, women were expected to be the maintainers and reproducers of the social power and political position of the *hamula*. In this social construct, women were defined, and defined themselves, solely as the mothers, sisters, wives and daughters of the males within the *hamula*. This property-related substitution of identity, to use Rossana Rossanda's words, was manifested in the class differences of Palestinian women's participation in the national resistance during the 1920s and 1930s.[8] During the peasant revolt of 1929 and the revolution of 1936-39, written history has accounted for the activism of one group of women only: those of the élite classes. The preposition 'of' here denotes the gender and class identities which these women appropriated during their political activism.

Using petitions, strikes, delegations to London and the well-known event of a 120-car parade of veiled women, they articulated their concerns through pleading for their husbands, sons, and fathers. Property forms, such as my son, my father, my family, and my husband have been substituted for women's identity. For example, the executive of the First Arab Women's Congress, then the major women's organization, contained the following names: 'President, Madame Dr Khalidi [the title Dr refers to the husband], Treasurer, Miss Shahinda Duzdar. Members: Mesdames Jamal Husseini, Mousa Alami, Owni Abdel Hadi, Shukry Deep ...'[9] Except for the treasurer, none of the women mentioned was designated by her own name; all were the daughters, wives and sisters of landowning families.[10]

Maintaining the status quo through reform rather than revolution to overthrow British colonialism and transform social relations was the aim of this movement. Thus, a memorandum sent by the First Arab Women's Congress (held in October 1929) read: 'We the Arab women of Palestine, having been faced with great economic and political difficulties and seeing that our cause has not so far received the sympathy and assistance of which it is worthy, have finally decided to support our men in this cause ...' Or 'The Arab Women's Congress sincerely hopes that your Excellency [the British governor] will be sympathetic to our cause and will assist us in the realization of our just and legitimate demands.'[11] It must be noted that 'our demands' refers to the demands of the Palestinian traditional national bourgeoisie. The problem with this form of women's activism and identity lies not only in its subsidiary and supportive character, for, as will be seen, the role of rural and poor women was not radically different. At issue is the role of class. By appropriating the culture of élite men, these women help to reproduce the culture of their own negation.

As far as the overwhelmingly rural society is concerned, Rossanda's assertion that: 'Power separates men from their companions more than poverty separates the male slave from the female slave; industry separates more than agriculture by dividing the "field" of presence', has some weight in the Palestinian context.[12] Like other Arab rural women, peasant women (fallahat) have never known the veil, were never secluded and always shared in the field as direct producers.[13] For rural women, the loss of land does not mean the loss of some social-class prestige — something they never had in the first place — it means the end of her and her children's lives. During the 1936-39 uprising, the guerrilla war that erupted throughout Palestine came largely from the rural areas. Despite the supportive character of women's political participation in this struggle, their role was life-risking.

While much of the economic dependency of the poor on the rich within the hamula was eroded under British and Zionist colonialism, the ideology of the heterosexual family and the subsidiary role of women remained largely intact. In fact, after the establishment of the state of Israel and the expulsion of over 80 per cent of the Palestinian people, women's marginal and subsidiary role took a historical twist. The slogan al-Ird Qablal Ard (Honour before Land) became a powerful cultural tool in responding to their expulsion, which was often accompanied by massacres of women and children, and rape.[14] Among Palestinian refugees in Lebanon the fusion between honour and cultural identity became very strong.[15]

For Palestinians in exile, it is not incomprehensible that the national cause and liberation superseded all other causes and liberations, such as those of class or gender. Nor is it incomprehensible that Palestinian women activists and militants from the Union of Palestinian Women (refugee women outside Palestine), in addressing International Women's Conferences, overemphasized their plight as a nation, even to the exclusion of their plight as women.[16]

Phase Two: 1949-67

REINFORCING traditional culture, despite the eradication of the material basis which gave rise to these traditions in the first place, is not peculiar to refugee camp collectives. The Palestinian minority in Israel, otherwise referred to as Arab Israelis, experienced similar conditions. Here, ironically, the same state which politically and legally tried to limit them numerically, has created objective conditions that strengthened their perceived need to expand demographically. Placed under military rule from 1949 until 1966, treated as second-class citizens, denied the right to social or political representation, Palestinians in Israel responded with a high birthrate. Whether these responses were economic in nature — as one social worker has explained to me — or a means to affirm their identity, there is no doubt that women were the major victims of this nationalist response. Painful means to induce miscarriage, such as carrying heavy items, were not unheard of.[17]

From military occupation to the 'Intifada'

THE third period in the participation of Palestinian women in the national struggle, from 1967 until today, provides a marked transformation in women's consciousness and organized activism, particularly for those in the *Intifada*. Before discussing the *Intifada*, however, a brief look at Palestinian women's conditions under 20 years of Israeli military occupation is worthwhile.

At the very least, mention should be made of the systematic expropriation by Israel of the major natural resources of the West Bank and Gaza Strip. More than 50 per cent of land in the West Bank and 60 per cent in the Gaza have been confiscated since 1967. Farmers in the Occupied Territories were denied access to water while water resources were diverted to the newly built Jewish settlements. The Israeli government imposed complete control over what, how, and when Palestinian farmers could plant. The Occupied Territories, with a population above 1.7 million, were turned into a consumer market for Israeli products. A process of forced proletarianization has produced a large reserve army of cheap Palestinian labour for use by Israeli capital and the state. Every day, more than 150,000 Palestinian labourers migrate to Israel looking for work. The atrocious working conditions of Palestinian labourers in Israel have been well documented.[18]

Israeli military rule has drained the Occupied Territories not only economically but politically and culturally. By banning trade unions, military rule has denied Palestinian workers the right to defend or even represent themselves. Attempts at political representation by the Palestinians were dealt with harshly by the Israelis. A vivid example is the assassination of the democratically elected mayors in the West Bank in the late 1970s. In fact, as far as political representation is concerned, Israel has repeatedly tried to interfere directly in the political process by creating an alternative leadership for the Palestinians. An example was the creation of the so-called Village League, a group of men who were armed, financed and fully supported by the Israeli military. Equally important to its economic and political repression of the Occupied Territories, Israel has also practised a policy of cultural deprivation. Palestinians were denied the right to organize as women or as students, or to establish any national or social institution. No Palestinian curriculum at schools or at universities was allowed. Israel intervenes in what is to be taught and who can teach at the Palestinian universities. Higher education institutions in general, and universities in particular, have often been targeted for closures following strikes or demonstrations. It is no surprise that Palestinians expend so much effort in reclaiming their cultural identity.

The Intifada, therefore, must be seen as not only an integral part of the continuum of the Palestinian national struggle, but also as the logical culmination of 20 years of military occupation.

It is undeniable that women's oppression cannot be isolated from the larger structural conditions under which they live. It is also true that their emancipation is dialectically linked to the emancipation and development of their society as a whole. But, what Palestinian women activists failed to do until the late 1970s was to show how to articulate women's emancipation with national emancipation. Until the late 1980s, Palestinian women in the Diaspora continued to give priority to the national struggle at the expense of their own cause.

Before articulating some of my findings around these issues, a methodological note is in order. I went into the field with a more or less clear understanding of what I intended to do and who I intended to meet. Organized women, women activists, and women in the leadership were the target. However, after a short stay in the West Bank, I realized that in order to get at the heart of the social and gender changes under way, I needed to speak to ordinary, non-organized women, both in the villages and in the refugee camps. Despite the difficulty of moving between camps and villages, which were often placed under curfew, I managed to visit various villages and refugee camps. The time that I spent with these women proved to be valuable, both theoretically and empirically.

Palestinian women's political uprising

THERE has been some documentation of the politicization of Palestinian women during the first two years of the *Intifada*. This includes data on women's political commitment and their determination to assume a vital role in the political process, suggesting a high level of political consciousness.[19] None the less, this process of women's political activism requires constant monitoring and analysis. Although the size and intensity of women's demonstrations have declined since the start of the *Intifada*, direct confrontations with the Israeli army by young people, and especially by women, remains a daily event. Confronting the Israeli army has become a self-conscious act which most women carry out fearlessly.

Young women in Ramalla and middle-aged and older women in Beit Sahour, for example, take pride in their brave stand in confronting Israeli military men. During my visit to an extended family household in Beit Sahour, the older woman in the house, and her three daughters-in-law, spoke of their utter indifference *vis-à-vis* Israeli armed men. In this particular household, where none of the members had any significant formal education, the atmosphere was distinctly self-confident.

The forms of women's confrontation include, but are not limited to, demonstrations and stone-throwing. The detention of over 17,000 men of all ages has left women with many added responsibilities.[20] When Beit Sahour villagers refused to pay taxes to military officials it was the women who opposed the collective punishment and house raids. The following story was told about one such raid:

A number of tax officials accompanied by military men raided a newly furnished house and wanted to collect a large amount of money. Upon their forced entry, they told the housewife that if she agreed to pay them only one shekel (less than 50 cents), they would waive all her taxes and leave the house. But the woman, abiding by what she perceives as the collective decision of the village, refused their request. For some hours, the woman stood silently watching the military men confiscating all her furniture and emptying her house. When they finished their mission the woman followed them with a side-table reminding them not to forget the last piece of furniture in her house.[21]

Women's confrontation with Israeli officials is also prevalent among refugee women in Israeli military courts. On one trip from Ramalla to Jerusalem I met a refugee woman who had just returned from the military court where she had been asked to bail her son out of prison. But she had refused to pay the court. When asked about her refusal to bail her son, she said:

I told the judge, in Arabic ... I am not sure if he understood, nor do I care ... Listen Judge! I am from Al-Jalazoun [refugee camp], I have seven children. You have detained three, one for the third time, and now you are asking for the fourth ... I will not pay you even one shekel ... Where I live is not better than where my sons are ... I know if you free him today you will detain him again tomorrow ... I will not reward you for what you are doing to us.[22]

Similar stories of women's national-political consciousness are found in almost every town, village and refugee camp. There is no doubt that confrontation with the Israeli authorities throughout the years of occupation, and the daily confrontations of the past three years, have escalated the political consciousness of the Palestinian masses. Moreover, one of the most striking features of the *Intifada* is the high level of organization to which most people appear committed. Despite the absence of a state apparatus, there appears to be a popular consensus around the directives issued in bi-monthly communiqués by the Unified Leadership of the *Intifada*. Daily commercial strikes, demonstrations, and confrontations with the Israeli army have become part of normal life in the Occupied Territories. But has this political-national awareness been accompanied by social-gender awareness? It is to this issue that we now turn.

Women's organization

THE phenomenon of women's organizations in the Occupied Territories, particularly in the West Bank, is not new. All four women's organizations or Committees (known as *utors*) were established during the late 1970s. The four *utors* were initially established as the women's wings of the four major political parties within the PLO with a primary goal to mobilize women politically. However, during the *Intifada*, a dramatic change occurred in the quantitative and qualitative structure of these *utors*. Although none of them was able to provide documented evidence of the extent of its membership, the Federation of the Women's Action Committees estimated its membership in the second year of the *Intifada* at 10,000 women. A representative from the Palestinian Women's Committees suggested that their membership exceeds 10,000.

Notwithstanding the vagueness of these statistics, what is clear is the existence of an organized women's movement mainly in the towns, but also in the villages and the refugee camps in the West Bank. (The situation in the Gaza Strip is different and will be addressed below.) Each of the four women's *utors* works separately. In major events, such as demonstrations, strikes, or a special collective response to a national or international event, the groups co-ordinate their activities. Common services and activities of the women's *utors* include providing day-care centres; organizing a social support network among women — particularly for those under stress; organizing literacy campaigns in the villages and refugee camps; and organizing community health education. In 1988, following the declaration of the independent Palestinian state, an attempt was made to unify all women's *utors* through the Higher Council of Women's Committees. For various reasons this was not successful.

Overcoming the lack of economic independence among the Palestinian community in general, and women in particular, was the major goal of the development enterprises and projects established by the women's committees. Of the four women's groups, two — the Federation of Women's Action Committees and the Palestinian Women's Committee — have been actively involved in promoting co-operatives for women. The declared aim of these projects is to enhance women's economic independence and provide 'the necessary steps towards their liberation'. Organizers in both committees strongly believe that, until women take an active part in the production process, all attempts at their liberation will be in vain.

Most of the economic development and income-generating co-operative projects involve food preparation, food processing and clothing. Other co-operatives involve small-scale industrial activity, such as the Copper Carving project in the West Bank village of Al-Isawiyeh. The idea of the co-operatives, as one organizer explained, emerged partly as a response to the boycott of

Israeli products, and partly as a means to enhance an economy of self-sufficiency among the Palestinians. These co-operatives are built within the context of the home economy. They involve an average of six women each and are established in the home. During the first two years of the *Intifada*, when the work of the popular committees and the neighbourhood committees was flourishing — a military order has since banned all popular and neighbourhood committees — these co-operatives were widespread throughout the West Bank. Each co-operative specialized in the production or processing of one product. Thus, in areas near citrus plantations, citrus juices are produced; grape juice and jams are manufactured in villages where grapes are grown.

Is there a socialist element in the co-operatives? In fact, organizers of these forms of activities see them as ideal for class and gender liberation. One activist stated: 'In the context of a traditional society where most of our women spend their time at home, these co-operatives are a big step forward ... women take part in the production process, they develop marketing skills, they feel they are a productive part in their society ...' [23] These projects not only pave the way for women's economic independence but also provide a learning experience in alternative economy.

It is well and good that women activists are involved in a process of building (or at least, planting the seeds for) an alternative economy. But it is doubtful that household co-operatives help to liberate women, for they place them in traditional domestic roles. After three years of experimenting with these co-operatives, some women activists began to debate their usefulness and emancipatory potential. Activists who accept the national symbolism of these projects — Palestinian goods versus Israeli products — argue that there is very little economic and social value in co-operatives. Returns from these small-scale enterprises are of very little economic value. A sharp criticism of the social-gender implications of co-operatives came from one activist from Beit Hanoun (Gaza), who put it this way: 'We and our mothers in this village are already overburdened with the household chores ... more work in the house means our double exploitation and further isolation from the outside world.' [24] Despite this criticism, women's co-operatives remain largely intact. Household co-operatives are still defended as important national enterprises and important achievements by women.

A more recent project, Beitello (named after a West Bank village) appears to be a step in the right direction. Established in the summer of 1989, the Beitello co-operative brings together fifteen to seventeen women. Multiple food items are produced and the work is done outside the home. Since production, managing, accounting, and marketing are undertaken by the workers themselves, it is likely that this experiment will prove more beneficial to the women involved than the small-scale, home-based enterprises.

The organized efforts at promoting women's economic independence carry with them the seeds for women's liberation. But, what needs to be carefully considered, as women, is who are we most interested in serving? Is it the national economy or women's economic independence? This question has not yet been answered. In discussions with the organizers of the various women's projects and co-operatives, I was led to believe that even the organizers continue to prioritize national aims over women's liberation. One co-operative's organizer put it bluntly: 'You have to understand that it is easier to organize women around national issues than around their own cause as women.' A similar response came from the manager of the Copper Carving project, who perceived the aim of their project as national, arguing: 'It is very important for us to preserve our culture ...'[25] There remains resistance to the idea that women's concerns must be given an independent weight and considered equally with national-political liberation.

Gender socialization and the women's movement

IS THE *Intifada* bringing about fundamental social change among Palestinians? Many of the traditional cultural practices and particularly the most repressive ones have begun to disappear. Darweish mentions the declining importance of lavishness and expenditure on marriages, the elimination of dowry, and the replacement of arranged marriage by marriage of individual choice.[26] What I would add is the meaning people give to some of these changes. For example, as regards marriage by choice among politically active people, I learnt that, since the *Intifada*, more than twenty-five cases of inter-religious marriages (between Muslims and Christians) have taken place in the Ramalla area. In some cases, men and women from the leadership had to intervene to convince the parents of the couple. Such a cultural change carries the seeds of a future secular society. Of course, inter-religious marriage among Palestinians is not widespread and is limited to a certain stratum. Moreover, this practice appears to be motivated by politics rather than the 'normal' course of social change.

As for weddings, there are fewer ostentatious and expensive ceremonies and the brideprice has disappeared in many cases. What remain are class distinctions among the Palestinians. The big bourgeoisie in Gaza and the West Bank continue to enjoy a lavish lifestyle and conduct their social affairs in the old manner, but the changes in wedding ceremonies are not welcomed by everyone in the villages and refugee camps. Traditionally, wedding preparations are the most important social events in the village. When women in Beit Sahour and Beit Hanoun (Gaza) were asked about this change, one middle-aged woman responded sadly: 'We forgot the joy of weddings ... Our weddings turned into mourning events ... Before the *Intifada*, all the village used to know about a wedding ... We all used to pitch in and help ... Now, she [the bride] leaves her house as if she were dragged to her grave ...' [27] It should be clear that social changes are perceived and experienced differently according to class, generation, and political consciousness; rural and urban dwellers also experience change differently. In any event, it appears that both the inter-marriage phenomenon and the changes in wedding ceremonies are conjunctural products of the intense political period rather than a permanent socio-cultural change.

The *Intifada* continues to bring to the fore a number of social contradictions, particularly around gender relations. For example, in Arab culture, the topic of sex and sexual relations is a social taboo. Sex-related issues cannot be discussed in public even if they are of criminal nature, such as rape. For women, sexual relationships before or outside marriage are prohibited. The rapes and sexual harassment of Palestinian women during the establishment of the state of Israel resulted in further restrictions on the women's movement, particularly among refugees. However, as early as the mid-1970s and with the political mobilization of many women, street demonstrators began to raise the slogan, *al-Ard Qablal Ird*, meaning land (or national freedom) before honour.

During the *Intifada*, the issue of honour was further politicized. A number of women, mainly in refugee camps and villages, were raped or sexually harassed by Israeli soldiers or by Palestinian collaborators. At the beginning of the *Intifada* these events were covered up or dealt with in utmost secrecy. Now, some political rapes have been dealt with by the *utors*, and even the Unified National Leadership has intervened. By bringing this issue to the fore, rape is being treated not as a matter of honour but as a political issue of public concern. Unfortunately, only political rapes are confronted. Secrecy surrounds social rapes, such as incest rapes, and to speak of them is taboo.

The *Intifada* has led to a slight relaxation in codes of women's behaviour. Sometimes this takes the form of an innovative method of hiding *shabab* (young Palestinian men) from the Israeli army. One woman told how she once saved a boy who was being followed by the army by allowing him to have a shower along with her daughter in order to hide his whereabouts. She explained that while the honour of her daughter was the most precious thing for her, the national cause was more important at that time.

That social-gender consciousness lags behind national-political awareness was most obvious in a meeting in July 1990 with representatives of the three largest women's committees in Beit Sahour. In the context of discussing women's liberation, the issue arose of possible changes within the household. One older woman said: 'I can go any time and attend any meeting ... My husband does not mind my wearing pants ... In fact, he often encourages me to go and he takes care of the children and of food ...' A second woman, carrying her baby in her arms, nodded in agreement. A third woman who was coming from the kitchen carrying coffee disagreed: 'No', she said, 'the woman has not yet taken her rights ... She is still not liberated ... I know that at home you will be washing dishes and your husband will be standing near the fridge asking you for a cold drink ...' She continued: 'If we women have achieved certain things it is because of us and our determination ... Our men are still traditional and our job remains to liberate them...' [28]

Surprisingly, the most critical discussion I had around male-female relations was with women in the Gaza Strip. Notwithstanding a state of absolute poverty, over-population, and great despair, activist women and men evince a sharp sense of social criticism. In Beit Hanoun (Gaza) I visited 'Fatima' in her parents' house. [29] When I arrived, family members and friends from both sexes and various age-groups were sitting together. All the women in this house — indeed, most women in the village — are unveiled. When we began our discussion, Fatima, Ameena, and Khaled stayed in the room. Unlike discussions held elsewhere, Fatima did not start with women's political changes but with herself. She asserted:

Women are strong, we don't need the men to educate us or read to us about politics ... We live politics ... We need men just to understand us and not to interfere in our choices ... I remember when I stood against my older brother and chose the man I wanted to be with. I knew then that I hurt my brother

because I took away one of his traditional roles. But at the same time I also
knew that I made him respect me more and treat me on equal footing to any
man in the village.

Ameena agreed, adding:

The double standards of our society and of our men really bother me. No
matter how politically committed you are, men still expect you to be a
perfect mother, a perfect wife and a perfect traditional woman ... I live in my
own house, but less than one block from my mother's house. I was able to
convince my mother that I have my own life to live. But, the neighbours still
can't understand why I don't visit my mother every day. [30]

My trip to Gaza convinced me of the need to discuss one issue which
could not have arisen in my stay in Jerusalem, Ramalla, Beit Sahour, or other
West Bank towns. This is the issue of Muslim fundamentalism, its impact on the
women's movement and the latter's responses to it.

Muslim fundamentalism and the women's movement

ONE activist from Gaza warned against overstating the extent of Muslim
fundamentalism and its impact on the *Intifada*. He complained that Israeli and
the Western media have used *Hamas* (the Islamist movement) and women's
veiling as means to distort the unity and strength of the *Intifada*. Although there
may be some validity to these assertions, they must be examined critically.

The spread of religious movements, particularly Islam in the Middle
East, is undeniable, especially after the Khomeini phenomenon in Iran. Those
who study Islamist movements need to explain why they are strong contenders
in some places but do not gain strength in others. With regard to the Occupied
Territories one might ask why the religious movement is widespread in the Gaza
Strip but not in the West Bank. The reasons are multiple and varied. Economically, geographically and demographically, Gaza is structured differently from
the West Bank. In the first instance, the Gaza·Strip is extraordinarily densely
populated — more than 70 per cent of its population are refugees. Much of the
land not confiscated by Israel is owned by a very small class of landowners. Economically underdeveloped, the Strip is not as important geopolitically as the

West Bank. There is a widespread feeling in Gaza that the area has been economically and politically marginalized by the Palestinian leadership, whether at the level of the PLO, the Unified Leadership, or the women's organizations. The *Intifada* has been especially strong in the Gaza Strip. To date, over 70 per cent of all detainees in Ansar 3 (Itzion prison in the desert) are from the Strip. Most of the documented cases of Israeli brutality, as well as rape, sexual harassment, and molestation are from the Gaza Strip.

It is my analysis that given the Gaza's marginalization and extreme poverty, and in the absence of a political solution to these hardships, a state of despair (*ihbat*) set in which proved fertile ground for a religious movement. One Marxist activist told me: 'I myself went to religion for three years. I put on the beard and spent most of my time in the houses of Sheikhs.' When asked why, he responded:

> In the late 1970s, after finishing my university degree I went back to my village in Gaza ... For a long time I was without work. There was nothing I could do. No books to read. Nowhere to go, just eat and sleep. People can't live by eating and sleeping alone. I decided to grow a beard and go religious. At the time I felt I was living for something, my life began to have meaning.

What had changed his mind?

> In the 1980s and after the Israeli invasion of Lebanon, a new life came back to Gaza ... that of resistance. Now with the *Intifada*, I feel I am regaining my pride as a human being ...[31]

Living a religious life as a mode of political resistance is not peculiar to the Gaza Strip. Saad Eddin Ibrahim's in-depth study of this phenomenon in Egypt provided a similar explanation.[32]

In terms of the effects of the religious revival on women, the issue is more complex. *Hamas* is not presenting itself as a religious movement only, it is also a political movement. In order to affirm itself on the ground and achieve recognition as a political power, the movement does not hesitate to use force. To appear as a dominant movement, *Hamas* tries to enforce religious symbolism in the streets. Most obvious is the veiling of women. Women have been beaten in the streets of Gaza for not wearing the veil, and have had tomatoes and bottles thrown at them for the same reason. On our way from Gaza town to Beit Hanoun, our car — a local car — was stopped three times by young boys. Although the driver introduced me as a journalist (without my permission), the car was not spared from being stoned. When I looked out from the window, a small boy, sitting with other boys, shouted at me: 'Cover your head!' I began to argue, but then I decided I had better things to do ... I covered my head!

In Beit Hanoun, neither Fatima nor Ameena was veiled, yet each had a different understanding of how veiling should be treated. According to Ameena: 'I am an activist and I will always want to be out working. If not wearing the *hijab* is going to restrict my movement, I don't mind putting it on. Here I am with you and unveiled ... Yesterday I was in the town and I had the veil on my head, I encountered no problems moving. When I come back to my village I take the veil off.'

Fatima disagreed. 'No ... you have to understand that what they want is not the *hijab* alone. They start by imposing the *hijab* on you, then enforce the *jilbab* [the long religious dress] and end up pushing us back home ... I am afraid that, next, women will not be permitted to leave their home except when they die or give birth ...' Then she burst out laughing adding: 'Even giving birth in hospitals might not be allowed.' Everyone in the room laughed for a moment, then she loudly said: 'What happened in Algiers will not be allowed to happen to us here ... We have gone a long way. They should not be allowed to stop us.'

When asked who could stop them, both Fatima and Ameena put the responsibility on the leaders at all levels. Ameena said: 'The problem cannot be solved at the individual level ... We in Beit Hanoun have solved the problem. We move around within the village unveiled and no one says anything. But here people know each other and family relations help. What about women in larger areas who have no family support behind them?' Fatima, Ameena and the men who entered the room during the conversation agreed that the Unified Leadership of the *Intifada*, with the full backing of the PLO outside, must act on this issue swiftly and immediately.

Women who pursue the issue of the veil seriously are disappointed with the way Palestinian political parties have treated the issue. Forces on the left, which include the three largest women's committees, have largely ignored or marginalized the problem. Nationalists who belong to the Fateh organization have, on a number of occasions, given in to *Hamas*. Women were encouraged — or more accurately ordered — to wear veils. Some women argue that Fateh uses this tactic partly to keep its women in the streets and partly to avoid an internal confrontation between the religious and the secular segments of the population. Whatever the reasons, the Palestinian national leadership — both its socialist and nationalist wings — must stand up against this socially reactionary movement.

Before leaving this issue two observations need to be made. The problem, as Gazan women correctly perceive it, is not one of *hijab* or *jilbab*. Veiling in Gaza is not volitional, as Saad Eddin Ibrahim claims it is in the Egyptian case. Women in Gaza are not given the choice of wearing or not wearing — this dress code is imposed on them. Two active Gazan women who chose to quit their committee over the issue of *hijab* pointed out that most young women who follow the religious directives are not themselves religious; they do it because they are under social or family pressures. As one woman put it, sarcastically: 'In the streets of Gaza, you see young women wearing the *hijab* while underneath they have a face which resembles a box of freshly cut vegetables ...'

Indeed, very few women wear the white or the dark 'correct' religious dress. Most *jilbabs* I saw were of different colours, cloth, and styles. The same applies to the *hijab*; they come in all colours and some are silk, others cotton. Finally, the class component of this phenomenon needs to be addressed. Upper-class women in Gaza enjoy a certain immunity from all this. As one woman put it: 'They hide in their big cars and no one attacks them or throws stones at them.'[33]

Before I left the West Bank in the summer of 1990, I was handed an important working paper on the dangers of fundamentalism, prepared by the Women's Study Committee at Bisan Research and Development Centre. The centre was preparing for a wide-scale public debate to discuss the 'phenomenon of force and imposition of the *hijab* and to prepare for strategies to fight this phenomenon'. During the *Intifada* a number of women's research and study centres emerged. One is the Women's Resource and Research Centre, which, according to its director, Dr Suha Hindiyeh, is dealing with women and Muslim law. The centre is preparing a study on how to modify or change the Personal Status laws. Some of the issues under study, Dr Hindiyeh said, include polygamy, women's property rights, her right to work, study, and her right to choose her marriage partner.

Conclusion

THIS chapter has explored the complexities of the gender-social transformation among women undergoing a national liberation struggle. I have tried to show that the *Intifada* has intensified women's political activism in almost all of Occupied Palestine. Refugee, village, and urban women have been intensely involved in the *Intifada*. Their activism and sacrifices are disputed by no one. NO GOING BACK is not an overstatement of the *Intifada*. What has been built on both the political-national front and the gender-social front cannot be reversed. The women's movement, particularly in the West Bank, is actively involved in building a new and equitable Palestinian society. Despite this, Palestinian women have a long way to go still to gain their rights fully.

The movement confronts many difficulties. Because of the anonymity of those who compose the Unified National Leadership, it is hard to assess the degree of autonomy of the four women's *utors*. Can it be that the absence of a genuine interest among the women's committees in fighting the issue is linked to the dependence of these committees on the higher echelons of the male leadership of the *Intifada*? This feeling was confirmed by Eileen Kuttab, a sociology lecturer at Bir Zeit University, who, along with other intellectuals and activists, has begun to realize the seriousness of the problem.

Discussions with grassroots women tend to suggest the presence of serious structural problems within the women's committees. Hanan Mikhail-Ashrawi has asserted that: 'Women's activity in the uprising has removed the basis of authority of the male. Traditional hierarchies are challenged by new hierarchies.'[34] But this is only partially true, for while male authority has been undermined to some extent, social class differences among the Palestinians are reflected in the women's movement. The middle-class character of the leadership of women's committees may be an obstacle to leading a popular movement. The Palestinian women's movement must avoid falling into the trap of institutionalization.

To maintain and develop the popular struggle, Palestinian women must face the challenge of inventing more adequate means of communication and organization. One needs to remember that the religious movement within the Algerian revolution emerged only towards the end of the struggle. After liberation it was able to manifest itself as a real power. Palestinian women need to seize the opportunity and act immediately, not only to affirm their presence in the *Intifada*: they also need to impose themselves at the higher levels of the general Palestinian leadership.

This research would not have been possible without the Palestinian women and men who made, and continue to make, the *Intifada*. The *Intifada* would not have survived had it not been for the many children, women and men who gave their lives, hopes and dreams for others to hope and work for a free life. My gratitude goes to all of my people.

It is painful to me that many women must remain anonymous for security reasons. Yet, I would like to thank the women of Beit Hanoun (Gaza Strip) and Beit Sahour (the West Bank) for the warmth and enthusiasm they demonstrated while I was with them. My special thanks go to Amal Moammar, Haifa As'ad and Maha Sabbagh who organized several meetings and made it possible for me to visit women's co-operatives. Together with these women I shall work for NO GOING BACK.

Notes

1. Benedict Anderson, *Imagined Communities: Reflections on the Origin and Spread of Nationalism* (London: Verso, 1983), p. 13.

2. Deborah Gaitskell and Elaine Unterhalter, 'Mothers of the Nation: A Comparative Analysis of Nation, Race and Motherhood in Afrikaner Nationalism and the African National Congress', in Floya Anthias and Nira Yuval-Davis (eds.) *Woman-Nation-State* (London: Macmillan, 1989), pp. 58-78.

3. Nira Yuval-Davis, 'National Reproduction and the Demographic Race in Israel', in Yuval-Davis and Anthias (eds.) *Woman-Nation-State*, p. 94.

4. Ibid., p. 96.

5. Quoted in Yuval-Davis and Anthias (eds.) *Women-Nation-State*, pp. 64, 67.

6. bell hooks, 'Political Solidarity Between Women', *Feminist Review* 21 and 23, 1986; Betsy Hartman, *Reproductive Rights and Wrongs* (New York: Harper and Row Publishers, 1987).

7. Nahla Abdo, *Women, Family and Social Change in the Middle East: The Palestinian Case* (Toronto: Canadian Scholarship Press, 1987); Abdo, *Colonial Capitalism and Rural Class Formation: A Case Study in the Social, Political and Economic Transformation of the Palestinians, 1920-47* (Toronto: University of Toronto, Department of Sociology, 1989), (unpublished PhD dissertation).

8. Rossana Rossanda, 'A Feminist Culture', in Monique Gadant (ed.) *Women of the*

Mediterranean (London: Zed Press, 1986), p. 191.

9. Matiel Mughannam, *The Arab Woman and the Palestinian Problem* (London: Hyperion, 1976), p. 76.

10. Abdo, op. cit., p. 21.

11. Mughannam, op. cit., pp. 74-5.

12. Rossanda, op. cit., p. 191.

13. Abdo, *Colonial Capitalism*.

14. Abdo, *Women, Family and Social Change*.

15. Ghazi al-Khalili, *The Palestinian Woman and Revolution* (Beirut: Palestine Research Centre, 1977) (in Arabic).

16. See conference reports, World Congress of Women, Moscow(11-14 May 1987).

17. Miscarriages from carrying heavy items or drinking bitter herbs were familiar in Nazareth where I grew up. I recall a pregnant woman moving a heavy sewing machine from place to place. Next day she told me she 'ended her pregnancy in the bathroom'.

18. Susan Rockwell, 'Palestinian Women Workers in the Israeli Occupied Gaza Strip', *Journal of Palestine Studies* XIV (2) (1985):114-36; Meron Benvenisti and Shlomo Khayat, *The West Bank and Gaza Atlas* (Jerusalem: West Bank Data Base, 1988).

19. Marwan Darweish, 'The *Intifada*: Social Change', *Race and Class* 31 (2), (October-December 1989), pp. 47-61; Rita Giacaman and Penny Johnson, 'Building Barricades and Breaking Barriers', pp. 155-69 in Zachary Lockman and Joel Beinin (eds.) *Intifada: The Palestinian Uprising Against Israeli Occupation* (Boston: South End Press, 1989).

20. See Database Project on Palestinian Human Rights 1988-90 (Chicago: Palestine Human Rights Information, Centre, 1990).

21. Interview in Beit Sahour, June 1990.

22. From Ramalla to Jerusalem, June 1990.

23. Interview with a group of women activists, Jerusalem, June 1990.

24. Interview, Beit Hanoun, Gaza Strip, June 1990.

25. Visit to the Copper Carving project, June 1990.

26. Darweish, op. cit., p. 59.

27. Interview, Beit Sahour, the West Bank, June 1990.

28. Interview with representatives of the Women's *Utors* (organizations), Beit Sahour, the West Bank, July 1990.

29. All names have been changed to protect privacy.

30. Interview, Beit Hanoun, Gaza Strip, June 1990.

31. Interview with a Gazan man, Gaza, June 1990.

32. Saad Eddin Ibrahim, *The New Arab Social Order: A Study of the Social Impact of Oil Wealth* (Boulder, Colo: Westview Press, 1982).

33. Interview, Gaza, June 1990.

34. Quoted in Giacaman and Johnson, op. cit., p. 160.

Selected Bibliography

Abdo, Nahla (1987) *Women, Family and Social Change in the Middle East: The Palestinian Case*, Toronto: Canadian Scholarship Press.

Afshar, Haleh, (ed.) (1987) *Women, State and Ideology in the Third World*, London: Macmillan.

Ahmad, J Al-e (1964) *Gharbzadegi*, Tehran (in Persian).

Akbar, Mansoor (1989) 'Revolutionary Changes and Social Resistance in Afghanistan', *Asian Profile* Vol. 17, No. 3, (June), pp. 271-81.

Amrane, Djamila (1991) *Les Femmes Algériennes dans la Guerre*, Paris: Plon.

Anderson, Benedict (1983) *Imagined Communities: Reflections on the Origin and Spread of Nationalism*, London: Verso.

Beck, L and N Keddie (eds.) (1978) *Women in the Muslim World*, Cambridge, Mass: Harvard University Press.

Fanon, Frantz (1982) *Sociologie d'une Revolution*, Paris: Maspero (1st ed. 1959).

Gadant, Monique (ed.) (1986) *Women of the Mediterranean*, London: Zed Books.

Ghoussoub, Mai (1987) 'Feminism — or the Eternal Masculine — in the Arab World', *New Left Review* 161 (Jan-Feb), pp. 3-13.

Hammami, Rema and Martina Rieker (1988) 'Feminist Orientalism and Oriental Marxism', *New Left Review* 170 (July-August), pp. 93-106.

Hess, Beth and Myra Ferree (eds.) (1987) *Analyzing Gender*, Beverly Hills: Sage.

Higgins, Patricia (1985) 'Women in the Islamic Republic of Iran: Legal, Social and Ideological Changes', *Signs* Vol. 10, No. 3 (Spring), pp. 477-95.

Hiltermann, Joost (1991) *Behind the Intifada: Labor and Women's Movements in the Occupied Territories*, Princeton, NJ: Princeton University Press.

Jayawardena, Kumari (1986) *Feminism and Nationalism in the Third World*, London: Zed Books.

Kabeer, Naila (1988) 'Subordination and Struggle — Women in Afghanistan', *New Left Review* 168 (March-April), pp. 95-121.

Kamali, Mohammad Hashim (1985) *Law in Afghanistan: A Study of the Constitutions, Matrimonial Law and the Judiciary*, Leiden: E J Brill.

Kandiyoti, Deniz (ed.) (1991) *Women, Islam, and the State*, London: Macmillan.

Keddie, Nikki R (1990) 'The Past and Present of Women in the Muslim World', *Journal of World History*, Vol. 1, No. 1, pp. 77-108.

Keddie, Nikki R and Beth Baron (eds.) (1991) *Women in Middle Eastern History: Shifting Boundaries in Sex and Gender*, New Haven, Conn: Yale University Press.

Kimmel, Michael (1990) *Revolution: A Sociological Interpretation*, Cambridge, UK: Polity Press.

Knauss, Peter, (1987) *The Persistence of Patriarchy: Class, Gender and Ideology in Twentieth Century Algeria*, Boulder, Colo: Westview Press.

Kruks, Sonia, Rayna Rapp, and Marilyn B Young (eds.) (1989) *Promissory Notes: Women in the Transition to Socialism*, New York: Monthly Review Press.

Lajoinie, Simone Bailleau (1980) *Conditions de femmes en Afghanistan*, Paris: Notre Temps/Monde.

Lockman, Zachary and Joel Beinin (eds.) (1989) *Intifada: The Palestinian Uprising Against Israeli Occupation*, Boston: South End Press.

Male, Beverly, (1982) *Revolutionary Afghanistan*, New York: St. Martin's Press.

Mandelbaum, David (1988) *Women's Seclusion and Men's Honor*, Tucson: University of Arizona Press.

Massell, Gregory J (1972) *The Surrogate Proletariat: Muslim Women and Revolutionary Strategies in Soviet Central Asia*, 1919-1929, Princeton: Princeton University Press.

Mernissi, Fatima (1987) *Beyond the Veil: Male-Female Dynamics in Modern Muslim Society*, Bloomington: Indiana University Press.

Minces, Juliette (1982) *The House of Obedience*, London: Zed Books.

Moghadam, Valentine M (1993) *Modernizing Women: Gender and Social Change in the Middle East*, Boulder, Colo: Lynne Rienner Publishers.

Mohanty, C T, A Russo and L Torres (1991) *Third World Women and the Politics of Feminism*, Bloomington: Indiana University Press.

Molyneux, Maxine (1985) 'Legal Reform and Socialist Revolution in Democratic Yemen: Women and the Family', in *International Journal of Sociology of Law*, Vol. 13, pp. 147-72.

Mumtaz, Khawar and Farida Shaheed (1987) *Women of Pakistan: Two Steps Forward, One Step Back?* London: Zed Books.

Mutahhari, Murteza (1987) *On the Islamic Hijab*, Tehran: Islamic Propagation Organization.

Nashat, Guity (ed.) (1983) *Women and Revolution in Iran*, Boulder, Colo: Westview Press.

Parker, Andrew, Mary Russo, Doris Sommer, and Patricia Yaeger (eds.) (1992) *Nationalisms and Sexualities*, New York: Routledge.

Peteet, Julie (1991) *Gender in Crisis: Women and the Palestinian Resistance Movement*, New York: Columbia University Press.

Rowbotham, Sheila (1992) *Women in Movement: Feminism and Social Action*, London: Routledge.

Roy, Olivier (1990) *Islam and Resistance in Afghanistan*, Cambridge, UK: Cambridge University Press, 2nd edition.

Saadi, Nouredine (1991) *La Femme et la Loi en Algérie*, Casablanca: Edition le Fennec.

Sabbah, Fatna (1984) *Woman in the Muslim Unconscious*, New York: Pergamon Press.

Shahrani, M Nazif and Robert L Canfield (eds.) (1984) *Revolutions and Rebellions in Afghanistan: Anthropological Perspectives*, Berkeley, California: Institute of International Studies.

Tabari, Azar and Nahid Yeganeh (eds.) (1982) *In the Shadow of Islam: The Women's Movement in Iran*, London: Zed Press.

Toubia, Nahid (ed.) (1988) *Women of the Arab World*, London: Zed Books.

Utas, Bo (ed.) (1983) *Women in Islamic Society,* Copenhagen: Scandinavian Institute of Asian Studies.

Worsley, P (1984) *The Three Worlds: Culture and Development*, Chicago: University of Chicago Press.

Yuval-Davis, Nira and Floya Anthias (eds.) (1989) *Woman-Nation-State*, London: Macmillan.

About the contributors

Nahla Abdo was born in Bethlehem, is a Palestinian activist, and is based at the Department of Sociology and Anthropology, and the Centre for Immigration and Ethno-Cultural Studies, Carleton University, Ottawa, Canada. She is the author of *Family, Women and Social Change in the Middle East: The Palestinian Case* (Canadian Scholarship Press, 1987), and many other articles on gender and women in the Middle East. She is involved in critical research on feminism, nationalism and Muslim fundamentalism, and is active in grassroots movements in Canada, including the women's and anti-racist movements.

Cherifa Bouatta teaches social psychology at the University of Algiers. She is active in the women's and democratic movements in Algeria. In addition to her work on the Algerian *Moudjahidates*, she has collaborated with Doria Cherifati-Merabtine on representations of women in the writings of the Algerian Islamist organization, the FIS.

Doria Cherifati-Merabtine teaches social psychology at the University of Algiers, and is an activist on the left and in the women's movement in Algeria. In addition to her collaborative work with Cherifa Bouatta on the FIS, she has researched women's employment and poverty issues.

Valentine M Moghadam is Senior Research Fellow at the United Nations University's World Institute for Development Economics Research in Helsinki. Born in Iran, she has been active in the democratic and women's movements, and has published widely on Iran, Afghanistan, the Middle East, and social and development issues. She visited Afghanistan in January-February 1989.

Salma Sobhan studied law at Cambridge and was the first woman from Bangladesh to become a barrister. She has been Director of the Legal Literacy Programme at BRAC (1986-90). She is now active in the women's movement, and a founder member of Ain-o-Salish Kendra. She is the author of *The Legal Status of Women in Bangladesh* (1978) and co-author of *No Better Options? Industrial Women Workers in Bangladesh* (1990).

Nayereh Tohidi, born in Iran, has been active in the democratic and women's movements, and obtained a PhD in educational psychology from the University of Illinois. She has taught women's studies at the University of California, Los Angeles, and has published widely in English and Persian on women and fundamentalism. In 1991-92 she was a Fulbright scholar in Baku, Azerbaijan, and at present is a research associate at Harvard University's Divinity School.

Index